"*Sex in a Broken World* is a v
of sin and the even deeper po
and theologically informed b

Gerald Hiestand, Senior Associate Pastor, Calvary Memorial Church;
Executive Director, The Center for Pastor Theologians; author, *Sex,
Dating, and Relationships: A New Approach*

"Paul Tripp has dealt with many important issues common to Christians.
Now he takes up another, in his customarily engaging style. This time, he addresses what is perhaps the most important moral issue of the church today:
sexual brokenness."

Ronald J. DeHaas, CEO, Covenant Eyes, Inc.

"Paul Tripp's writing always challenges, encourages, and inspires me. *Sex in
a Broken World* did just that. Sexuality can be beautiful, but it's also broken,
so we have to be honest about the topic. If you read this book with an open
and humble heart, God will use it to deepen your passion for Christ and help
you discover a life of freedom, purity, and joy."

Craig Groeschel, Pastor, Life.Church; author, *Daily Power: 365 Days
of Fuel for Your Soul*

"Once again, Paul Tripp has graciously and pastorally applied the comfort
and challenge of the gospel to the street-level reality of our lives. This time,
with *Sex in a Broken World*, sexuality and relationships are unpacked and
explained in a way that leads readers to be gently discipled, not scolded or
made to feel shame. I am so grateful for a book that I can recommend to
women, who, like men, need the hope and wisdom of Christ applied to this
aspect of their humanity!"

Ellen Mary Dykas, Women's Ministry Coordinator, Harvest USA;
editor, *Sexual Sanity for Women*

"Lots of books are written about sex, but none of them are like this one. This
book is an unapologetically God-centered view of sex, exploring not only
how God intended it to work, but also why it so often does not. Paul Tripp,
who has to be one of our generation's most insightful Christian thinkers, asks
questions in this book that few people of faith dare to ask: Why did God
create me with unfulfilled desires? Why do I so often feel disappointed? What
does God really feel toward me when I fall to those same temptations again
and again? You will not only read this book, but you will devour it, and you'll
likely find yourself recommending it to everyone you know."

J. D. Grear, Pastor, The Summit Church, Raleigh-Durham, North
Carolina; author, *Not God Enough* and *Gospel: Recovering the Power
That Made Christianity Revolutionary*

"Sexual insanity has taken over our world, so we need sane counsel from a wise counselor. Paul points us to Christ, grounds us in truth, and navigates a pathway through the craziness. Would you expect anything less from Paul Tripp?"

Deepak Reju, Pastor of Biblical Counseling and Family Ministry, Capitol Hill Baptist Church, Washington, DC; author, *The Pastor and Counseling* and *She's Got the Wrong Guy*

"This is everything we've come to expect and appreciate from Paul Tripp's writing: searing realism about ourselves and unbounded confidence in the power of the gospel to bring insight, wisdom, and restoration. This is an urgently needed book and will be an eternal blessing to many."

Sam Allberry, Speaker, Ravi Zacharias International Ministries; author, *Is God Anti-Gay?*

"This wonderful book shines the bright hope of the gospel into the deep darkness of guilt and shame. Not simply scapegoating our post-Christian culture, Paul 'normalizes' a universal human struggle that afflicts every child of God. Like me, you will find yourself in these pages: assured you're not worse than others and that your loving, heavenly Father understands your weakness, offered up his Son to redeem your sexuality, and poured out his Spirit to empower your transformation. Join me in celebrating with Paul our great God who redeems broken things!"

David White, Director of Targeted Discipleship, Harvest USA; author, *Sexual Sanity for Men*

"Many books today confront the sexual brokenness of the modern world. Precious few equip you to spot counterfeit hopes while leaving you with an exhilarating sense of true hope. I know of no better antidote to our sexualized age than *Sex in a Broken World*. Read it, examine your own heart and habits, and soak in the renewing, restoring, overcoming grace of Jesus Christ."

Owen Strachan, Associate Professor of Christian Theology, Midwestern Baptist Theological Seminary; coauthor, *The Grand Design*; coeditor, *Designed for Joy*

Sex in a Broken World

Sex in a Broken World

How Christ Redeems What Sin Distorts

Paul David Tripp

CROSSWAY®

WHEATON, ILLINOIS

Adapted from *Sex and Money: Pleasures That Leave You Empty and Grace That Satisfies* (Wheaton, IL: Crossway, 2013), out of print.

Cover design: Jordan Singer

First printing 2018

Printed in the United States of America

Unless otherwise indicated, Scripture quotations are from the ESV® Bible (The Holy Bible, English Standard Version®), copyright © 2001 by Crossway, a publishing ministry of Good News Publishers. Used by permission. All rights reserved.

Scripture references marked NIV are taken from The Holy Bible, New International Version®, NIV®. Copyright © 1973, 1978, 1984, 2011 by Biblica, Inc.™ Used by permission. All rights reserved worldwide.

Trade paperback ISBN: 978-1-4335-5665-4
ePub ISBN: 978-1-4335-5668-5
PDF ISBN: 978-1-4335-5666-1
Mobipocket ISBN: 978-1-4335-5667-8

Library of Congress Cataloging-in-Publication Data

Names: Tripp, Paul David, 1950- author.
Title: Sex in a broken world : how Christ redeems what sin distorts / Paul David Tripp.
Description: Wheaton : Crossway, 2018. | Includes bibliographical references and index.
Identifiers: LCCN 2017014538 (print) | LCCN 2017045264 (ebook) | ISBN 9781433556661 (pdf) | ISBN 9781433556678 (mobi) | ISBN 9781433556685 (epub) | ISBN 9781433556654 (tp)
Subjects: LCSH: Sex—Religious aspects—Christianity.
Classification: LCC BT708 (ebook) | LCC BT708 .T733 2018 (print) | DDC 261.8/357—dc23
LC record available at https://lccn.loc.gov/2017014538

Crossway is a publishing ministry of Good News Publishers.

LB		28	27	26	25	24	23	22	21	20	19	18
15	14	13	12	11	10	9	8	7	6	5	4	3	2	1

For new morning mercies and daily rescuing grace
I am eternally grateful.

Contents

Preface

It's the afternoon following the morning that I finished the book you're now reading. The best description of my mood right now is that I am a sad celebrant. I am devastated at what this book has exposed in me. I am grieved by the lust that still resides in my heart, but I am far from hopeless, because writing this book has excited me at an even deeper level than ever before with the liberating and transforming power of the grace of the Lord Jesus.

I am sad to think that when it comes to sex, we still buy into the legalism that says if we can organize people's lives, give them the right set of rules, and attach them to efficient systems of accountability, we can deliver people from their sex insanity. The fact that we can look at the power of sexual sin to deceive and enslave people and feel comfortable in our reliance on the scant power of human intervention is itself insane. Few areas of the human struggle reveal more powerfully the sad sinfulness of sin than the sex evils that are done to people and through people hundreds of thousands of times every day. The delusion and confusion is so great that we cannot even agree anymore on how to define what were once commonly understood terms such as *sex* and *gender*.

Yet in the face of all this, there is still robust reason for joy. All over, the church of Jesus Christ is returning once again to the hope of the gospel. All over, Christian leaders young and old are looking to the gospel of Jesus Christ to help them diagnose sex problems, while at the same time holding out to those who are tempted, weak, or addicted the hope that is found only in the grace of Jesus.

Still, it is sad to think of how many people will look today to sex to give them what sex cannot give and, in so doing, give way to temptation and deepen their addiction. It is sad to think of how many people in their shame will deny the wrong of what they are doing and the depth of their enslavement. And while so many struggle in private, it is sad to see that the surrounding culture seems to get more and more sex insane with every passing day.

Yet in the face of all this, there is a happy rest in knowing that Jesus still reigns and will continue to advance the march of his kingdom until the last enemy is under his foot. He reigns over all the situations, locations, and relationships that would otherwise give you and me cause for despair. He reigns for his own glory and our good. And his reign is our guarantee that he will deliver all he has promised, because only he can guarantee he'll make good on his promises in the places he rules—by the way, that's everywhere.

So go ahead and read this book as a sad celebrant. I hope that at times it will bring you to tears and at other times cause you to shout for joy. Rejoice with a frown or celebrate with tears. It really is what we should be doing between the "already" and the "not yet," while we still wait with the assurance that our Messiah will bring our sex struggles to an end.

Paul David Tripp
October 11, 2012

1

Sex in a Broken World

She felt robbed. She was thirty, single, and in most ways very content except for one area of her life. She just couldn't understand why God would design her to be a sexual being with strong sexual desires and then forbid her to participate in and enjoy sex. She would see couples at the local gastropub snuggling in the corner, and the sight would fill her with an explosive combination of envy and anger. She had always been serious about her faith and tried to live it practically, but this sex thing was about to push her over the edge. More and more God seemed more of a harsh judge than someone who loved her. She thought, "How can I serve a God who hardwires me with desires and then tells me he'll discipline me if I fulfill them?" It left her depressed and confused.

- - -

Sharon knew that her son was messing around with sex, but she couldn't get him to admit it. She tried to get into his computer but didn't know his password. At times he would make an off-color comment or tell a joke with sexual overtones, and, every time, Sharon's heart would sink. They had tried to prepare him for life in this fallen world, but changes had come fast and hard, so much so that Sharon felt she was living in a world she herself no longer understood. Her son was never off his phone. He seemed always to be talking about a girl or texting a girl or going out somewhere with a girl. And when he was with a girl at home, Sharon felt that the interaction between them was too physical. It got so that Sharon hated sex—hated that God had created it, hated that her sixteen-year-old son already had strong sexual desires. She hated that sex talk was everywhere. She felt helpless and powerless; she thought she was losing her son, and there was nothing she could do.

—   —   —

She was fourteen, and she liked being sexy, but she didn't want her mom to know. She would leave for school in a parent-approved outfit but often with a "cooler" outfit in her book bag to change into at school. To her, a "cool" outfit was one designed to reveal the body rather than modestly cover it. Although most of her friends did the same, she knew her dad would kill her if he ever found out. She longed to be popular, and being popular meant getting lots of Facebook and Instagram likes, and the way to get likes was to be provocative. Her selfies became increasingly sexual. She hadn't posted anything nude, but the image she was projecting was intentionally sexually provocative. She was getting lots of attention from the boys at school and from "boys" on the Internet whom she didn't know. She was living a full-blown Kardashian fantasy, and she loved it. Her parents didn't have a clue, and if they had, they would've been heartbroken and gone ballistic at the same time. She was only fourteen, and sex is what drove her world.

- - -

He drove home that night with a heavy heart. The story he had already heard too many times, he had heard again today. He was depressed from pastoring people he couldn't seem to help. That day in his office he had talked to yet another couple whose marriage had been shattered by illicit sex. The wife cried and shed the tears of yet another betrayal. The man sort of confessed, but his confession was laden with excuses and the typical minimizing of what he had done. He seemed more mad that he had been caught than grateful that he had been rescued from the hold of something that had the power to destroy him. His sin had not only shattered his marriage, but lost him his job as well.

It was all so discouraging for the pastor to hear. He spoke to them of the grace of the gospel, but his heart wasn't in it. He once had confidence in the power of God, but his confidence had been weakened by the number of men in his church who had fallen into sexual sin. It not only weakened his confidence in God's grace, but it made him question his calling. Why in all his teaching, preaching, and counsel had he not been able to protect the men whom God had called him to pastor? It was hard to keep going when God seemed distant and when he felt like a failure. He knew that when he got home, his wife would ask about his day. He dreaded that question so much that he took the long way home. Sex was eating holes in his church, and there seemed to be no stopping it.

- - -

So, what's your story? You're probably reading this book because, like me, you're concerned. You're probably concerned because in the middle of the onslaught of all that our culture is saying about sex, you want to think about it in a distinctly biblical way. Or maybe you're concerned because you're raising children in a sexual culture that, frankly, scares you. Or perhaps you know people who have gotten into some sort of sexual trouble, and you'd like to understand what they're dealing with and how to offer them help that is truly helpful. Or maybe you're a pastor, and you want to teach your people well about an area of life that the church often fails to speak forthrightly and clearly about. Perhaps you're battling with sexual sin in your own life, and you feel defeated and hopeless.

If you're in any of those situations, this is what you need to understand: you live in a deeply broken world that simply does not function as God intended. If you want to understand the nature of sexual sin, or if you want to develop a biblical-sex worldview, you have to include this fact. Now, you may be thinking that this is an awfully negative way to start a book about sex, but here's my response: you will never completely understand our deep struggle with human sexuality unless you first understand the context or the environment in which that struggle takes place.

And Now for the Bad News

I can't think of a more descriptive, honest, insight-giving, and hopeful description of the present state of the world you live in, and how it affects areas of life such as human sexuality, than Romans 8:18–39. What follows is a lengthy quote, but take time to read it in full. As our discussion proceeds, you'll be glad you did.

> For I consider that the sufferings of this present time are not worth comparing with the glory that is to be revealed to us.

For the creation waits with eager longing for the revealing of the sons of God. For the creation was subjected to futility, not willingly, but because of him who subjected it, in hope that the creation itself will be set free from its bondage to corruption and obtain the freedom of the glory of the children of God. For we know that the whole creation has been groaning together in the pains of childbirth until now. And not only the creation, but we ourselves, who have the firstfruits of the Spirit, groan inwardly as we wait eagerly for adoption as sons, the redemption of our bodies. For in this hope we were saved. Now hope that is seen is not hope. For who hopes for what he sees? But if we hope for what we do not see, we wait for it with patience.

Likewise the Spirit helps us in our weakness. For we do not know what to pray for as we ought, but the Spirit himself intercedes for us with groanings too deep for words. And he who searches hearts knows what is the mind of the Spirit, because the Spirit intercedes for the saints according to the will of God. And we know that for those who love God all things work together for good, for those who are called according to his purpose. For those whom he foreknew he also predestined to be conformed to the image of his Son, in order that he might be the firstborn among many brothers. And those whom he predestined he also called, and those whom he called he also justified, and those whom he justified he also glorified.

What then shall we say to these things? If God is for us, who can be against us? He who did not spare his own Son but gave him up for us all, how will he not also with him graciously give us all things? Who shall bring any charge against God's elect? It is God who justifies. Who is to condemn? Christ Jesus is the one who died—more than that, who was raised— who is at the right hand of God, who indeed is interceding for us. Who shall separate us from the love of Christ? Shall tribulation, or distress, or persecution, or famine, or nakedness, or danger, or sword? As it is written,

> "For your sake we are being killed all the day long;
>   we are regarded as sheep to be slaughtered."

No, in all these things we are more than conquerors through him who loved us. For I am sure that neither death nor life, nor angels nor rulers, nor things present nor things to come, nor powers, nor height nor depth, nor anything else in all creation, will be able to separate us from the love of God in Christ Jesus our Lord. (Rom. 8:18–39)

This shocking, dark passage is also one of the most gloriously helpful and hopeful passages in the New Testament. The apostle Paul unpacks for us here the environment that we all live in between the already and the not yet. Take note of the foundational assumption that frames everything else he says in the passage (v. 18). Paul assumes that suffering is the universal experience of everyone living between the already and the not yet. If you begin to pay attention, you will realize that you and I never live a day without experiencing suffering of some kind. Suffering is not an indication that something alien or weird is happening to us. Suffering is not a sign that we have been singled out for abuse. Suffering is not a sign of the failure of God's rule, his plan, or his promises. Suffering is the natural experience of everyone who lives where you and I live. Rather than being shocked when trouble and difficulty enter our lives, we should be surprised how well this world works, given its condition.

If suffering is every person's experience, then you should expect suffering to impact your sexuality. You will suffer the reality that right here, right now, sex doesn't function the way that God intended. You will face the redefinition, distortion, and misuse of sex. You suffer the temptation to take your sexual life outside of God's clear boundaries. You will suffer being blindsided by sexual temptation at the mall, on your computer, when watching Netflix, or, sadly, even when you're doing a Google search on your phone. You will suffer women exposing their bodies in public or men treating women like they're little more than physical toys for their pleasure. You will suffer the hardship of trying to protect your children from all the sexual danger out there, while you work to keep your own heart pure. Because you know of all the seductive temptations, you will suffer issues of trust with those you love. Some of us will suffer sexual abuse, and others of us will suffer the exhaustion that comes from trying to keep our hearts pure. You will suffer misunderstanding and mockery as you try to stay inside God's boundaries in a culture that laughs at the thought of sexual boundaries. Paul assumes that we will suffer, and if he's right (and he is), that suffering will include our sexuality.

Why does Paul assume we will suffer? He assumes suffering because he understands the condition of the world in which God has chosen us to live (vv. 19–25). With graphic and provocative terminology, Paul wants us to understand that God has chosen to keep us right now in a terribly broken world, one that does not function in the way he intended. Again, our present address is not an interruption or failure of God's plan for us. Paul's way of capturing the brokenness of our world is to say that "the whole creation has been groaning." Picture the old man whose body is aged and broken, where even something as simple as getting out of a chair, bending to pick something up, or taking a few steps makes him audibly groan. That's our world. Nothing is simple anymore. Everything is affected by brokenness. There is no location or situation or sector of the world that does not groan.

If you don't understand your address, you will live with all kinds of unrealistic expectations, and you will be way too naïve about the myriad of temptations that greet you every day. And because your understanding and expectations of your environment are unrealistic, you will be functionally unprepared for the struggles you will inevitably face. You'd better understand, and help those entrusted to your care to understand, that the whole sex aspect of our world groans in sad and comprehensive brokenness. And you'd better understand that that brokenness doesn't live just outside you but inside you as well. This is important to get, because the brokenness inside will hook you to the sexual temptations outside.

You are a sexual being, but that aspect of your personhood lives not in a sexually healthy world but one that is deeply broken, and that changes everything. *Where, right now, is your sexual life groaning? Where, right now, are you facing the brokenness of the sexual world around you?*

There is one more aspect to Paul's description of our brokenness and the brokenness of the world around us. He says that this broken world is *waiting for redemption*. Governments can't fix this brokenness, institutions of higher learning can't fix it, and physicians can't fix it. This world and all its brokenness cry out for one thing: a redeemer. That redeemer is Christ, whose forgiving and transforming grace is the only hope for us, our world, and our sexual brokenness.

There are maybe few areas of our lives that preach more loudly to us of our need for redemption than our constant struggle with sex. When it comes to sex, the promises we make to ourselves and others tend to be short-lived. Our commitment to purity of heart and hands tends to weaken in the face of temptation. It doesn't take much for our eyes and our desires to wander. In the sexual arena we are confronted with the truth that we will never be righteous on our own. Sex preaches to us all that we deeply and desperately need grace.

Thankfully, in this passage it's not the brokenness of the world that dominates Paul's discussion, but grace. In a powerful and practical way, Romans 8:18–39 points us to the only place where we can find help and hope for our sexual brokenness. Grace offers us what we cannot do for ourselves. Grace offers us what changes of situation, location, and relationship will never give us. There is grace for every aspect of the sexual brokenness in and around us, and that really is the very good news of this passage.

The Best News Ever for Our Sexual Struggles

The question begged by dark honesty about our present address—identified in Romans 8—is this: What does God give us to face our inevitable struggles and sufferings? The resoundingly glorious answer of Romans 8 is that God does not give us this thing or that thing to help us. No, he gives us the only thing that can truly provide the rescue, wisdom, and strength we need. What is that one thing? I love saying this! God's best and most precious gift to us between the already and the not yet is the gift of himself. He doesn't promise a life free from struggle. He doesn't promise us that we will not suffer. He doesn't promise that our sexuality will be free from distortion and temptation. No, he promises us that in all these situations he will be with us, in us, and for us. God *is* the grace he offers us.

In fact, this passage carries with it one of the most powerful and concise definitions of God's presence and grace that you will ever find. It's there in verse 31: "If God is for us, who can be against us?" Where can hope for a healthy, godly, and morally pure sexual life be found? Here is the answer in three wonderful words, *God for us.* Let it echo in your mind: *God for us.* Let it ring in your heart: *God for us.* Let it shape the way you think about how to live God's way sexually in a world that ignores him and rejects his wise and loving plan. Let these words give you courage in the face of confusion, misunderstanding, and temptation. Let them give you hope when you feel defeated by sexual temptation. It's never us against the giant of seductive sexual allure, because by grace God really is for us.

So Romans 8 doesn't just alert us to the broken, groaning world we live in, but it points to God's presence with us and the grace he offers us. Let's examine this grace.

1. *God's grace is often uncomfortable grace* (Rom. 8:18–25). The difficulties we face in the here and now are not a sign that God has forgotten or abandoned us. He knows where he has placed us. He has placed us here because he is not after our ease; he is after our hearts. It is important that we embrace the theology of uncomfortable grace, because between the already and the not yet, God's grace comes to us in uncomfortable forms. Notice in the apostle's description of our groaning world are the words "hope" and "redemption." In the hands of our Redeemer, this broken, groaning world becomes a tool of his transforming, refining, heart-changing grace. God uses the sexual brokenness around us to expose our wandering hearts. No, he won't ever tempt us to sin, but he will use the sexual chaos around us to drive us to more deeply and consistently follow him. He is able and willing to turn what is broken and groaning into a tool of his grace.

2. *God's grace is intervening grace* (Rom. 8:26–27). At times the battle is so great, so discouraging, and so emotionally taxing that you don't even know how to pray. You've fallen again and focused your eyes on what God prohibits or used your body for what God has forbidden, and you feel so defeated. This passage says that in those moments, when the weakness is so deep, and you're distraught and confused—so much so that you don't know how to pray—God does not turn his back on you. No, the opposite is true. The Holy Spirit, who lives inside you, carries your intelligible cries in words of grace to the Father. He intervenes for you when you have no strength or ability to intervene for yourself.

3. God's grace is unstoppable grace (Rom. 8:28–30). I've had countless people say to me in counseling sessions, "I think I've fallen too much. I think I've wanted my way too much, and I sometimes think my life is in such a sorry state because God has given up on me." It is a cruel lie of the Enemy that God would ever give up on one of his blood-purchased children. Because my sex life exposes what a wandering heart I have, I need to know that the heart of my Redeemer will never, ever wander. This is exactly what these verses tell us, that God will absolutely finish the work of grace that he has begun in each of us. His grace is never at risk. His grace is never at stake. His grace is never up for grabs. His grace never waffles. Here's the vital message of these verses: *the grace you are receiving today is the present expression of a plan that was firmly set in place before the foundations of the world were laid.* Nothing or no one can stop the move of this grace.

4. God's grace is providing grace (Rom. 8:31–32). I love the logic of these verses. If God went to the extent of harnessing forces of nature and controlling the events of human history so that at just the right time his Son would come and live, die the death we should have died, and rise again, conquering sin and death, would it make any sense that God would abandon us along the way? The cross is our guarantee that in all our struggles with sex, no matter who we are and what those struggles may be, God will give us everything we need. If he willingly gave us his Son, we can rest assured he will gladly supply what we are not able to supply for ourselves.

5. God's grace is inseparable grace (Rom. 8:33–39). Finally, in case any doubt still remains about the presence and reliability of God's grace, Paul assures us that we will never encounter or struggle with anything that has the power to separate us from the love of the One who so generously blesses us with his presence and his grace. This world, with all its sexual distortion, confusion, and seduction, can't separate you from God's love. Your darkest moment of sexual wandering and defeat can't separate you from God's love. Your pride in your independent self-righteousness, where you take credit for what only God can produce, can't separate you from God's love. His love is eternal.

I decided to use Romans 8:18–39 as the launching pad for this book because it so graphically captures the zeal of what you're about to read. Romans 8 is stunningly honest in its description of the groaning world we live in and wonderfully hopeful about the realities of God's presence with us and grace for us. The honesty of Romans 8 doesn't negate its hope, and the hope doesn't weaken its honesty. And this is the way it should be. If what the Bible says is right about who God is and what he has given us in Jesus Christ, then we should be the most honest community on earth, because we know that whatever is known or exposed about us has already been fully covered by his amazing grace.

So take this journey of honesty and hope with me. I'm deeply persuaded that it is an essential journey, because, as I'm about to detail, when it comes to sex we've gone more than a bit crazy.

Review and Reflect

1. What aspect of our sexualized culture most concerns you? On a personal level, can you relate to any of the scenarios at the beginning of chapter 1? As you seek to answer those questions, why is it vital to grasp the reality that "you live in a deeply broken world that simply does not function as God intended" (p. 16)?

2. Reread Romans 8:18–39, which Paul Tripp describes as shocking and dark but also helpful and hopeful (p. 18). In what specific ways does the passage portray both sinful darkness and glorious hope? How does the passage inform our thinking about sexuality?

3. Paul Tripp writes, "If you don't understand your address, you will live with all kinds of unrealistic expectations" (p. 19). Explain what he means.

4. What is God's most precious gift to us for living life in our broken world?

5. Paul Tripp sheds light on the grace God offers us. Where in your own life have you seen the particular aspects of this grace:

   • uncomfortable grace

   • intervening grace

   • unstoppable grace

- providing grace

- inseparable grace

Heart Reset

- Romans 8:18–39

2

Sorry, but We've Gone Crazy

She's thirteen, and the thing she can't stop thinking and talking about is her impending breast development. For her, being a woman is all about the size of one's breasts.

She's fifteen and is quite the self-appointed expert when it comes to oral sex. She doesn't see herself as just knowledgeable but as a bit experienced as well. What she likes about oral sex is that it's a way of having sex that "isn't really sex."

I've told my wife that during the summer months it's hard to walk down the street in Center City Philadelphia, where we live, and to know where to look, because there are so many women in various stages of undress.

Tim is seventeen, and in ways he doesn't recognize, he's already been trained to view women as objects whose value is attached to physical beauty and body shape.

George is married with three children; he seems to have a good marriage, but he masturbates at least once a day. His wife doesn't know it, but he's done it for years.

They came to me after a conference, carrying with them a combination of heartbreak and anger. They wanted to know what to do about their son who seemed hopelessly addicted to Internet pornography. I asked how old he was, thinking I would hear teens or early twenties. To my shock, and speaking through his shame, the father said to me, "Eight." Eight! Let it sink in. Eight!

At a conference in South Africa they asked if they could have lunch with me. After the meal they told me their story. Their son, a newly married intern pastor, had been having sex with a college girl from the student ministry over which he was responsible.

In the big cities around the world, you are considered a hopelessly old-fashioned bigot if you don't think same-sex marriage is not only a wonderful idea but also a civil right.

We're now being told by powerful cultural influencers that gender is not a fixed biological reality but rather a cultural construct.

You can barely watch a video, look at a car ad, or hear a popular song without having your morals assaulted.

Sandra is twenty, and her definition of cool, fashionable clothes is those that are designed to reveal the body. Her clothes tend to be tight, short, and often low-cut. Sandra is a Christian who in many ways takes her faith seriously.

He asked to counsel with me because he knew he was in trouble. He was literally stalking women in the evenings after his seminary classes. He would hang around Starbucks and follow the most attractive women home, of course never letting them know what he was doing.

How many teachers, how many coaches, have been arrested for having sex with the students entrusted to their care?

There are websites that connect people who want to be unfaithful to others who are desirous of the same.

An inner-city high school opens up a day care next to the school building because so many of its female students have children.

So many people are texting sexually explicit pictures from their cell phones that the word *sexting* has become part of the modern vocabulary.

Internet pornography is the most powerful economic engine of the World Wide Web.

- - -

Sex—you don't have to look very far to see that we're in big trouble. The news is littered daily with sex scandals. The content of the tabloids is enough to alert us to the fact that something has gone terribly wrong. It's hard to listen to any cultural discussion of sex that isn't infected with either self-deception or distortion of reality. Sex can't deliver the promise that we think it makes, and it's more dangerous than we tend to think. Sadly, today this beautiful creation of God functions in the surrounding culture like a spiritual solvent eating away at the very fabric of the human community. It has perverse power to master your heart and, in so doing, determine the direction of your life. It gives the buzz that you're in control while, at the very same time, becoming the master that progressively chains you to its control. It offers you an inner sense of well-being while having no capacity whatsoever to satisfy your heart. It seduces you with the prospect of contentment-producing pleasure but leaves you empty and craving more. Sex holds out the possibility that you will finally be satisfied but instead causes you to envy whoever has more and better than you do. It sells you the lie that physical pleasure is the pathway to spiritual peace. Sex is the work of the Creator's hands but tends to promise you what only the Creator can deliver. It is beautiful in itself but has become distorted and dangerous by means of the fall.

With all of this swirling around us and inside us, the church of Jesus Christ has been strangely silent and reticent. We seem to approach sex with a timidity, reserve, and embarrassment that does not make personal, cultural, or biblical sense. Pastors are often all too hesitant to teach and preach about the topic of sex. Meanwhile, the world around us seems to never stop talking about it.

Christian parents often fail to do a good job of discipling their children in what it means to be God-honoring sexual beings. How many parents do more than conduct one creepy, quasi-embarrassing talk about sex and have joy once it's over and a determination never to talk about it again? How many young people from Christian homes are struggling with questions, confusion, and temptation but wouldn't think of seeking the help and wisdom of their embarrassed and silent parents? How many parents provide a long-term, safe, gracious, and nonjudgmental place for their teens to talk about sex, knowing that the questions and temptations of a thirteen-year-old differ from those of a fifteen-year-old, which differ from those of an eighteen-year-old? Meanwhile, the obsessions and distortions of an addicted culture are powerfully brought to the eyes, ears, and hearts of even the most conservative Christians by pervasive and intrusive media that is almost impossible to escape.

Yet God in his great wisdom, for his glory and our good,

has chosen to place us in a world where sex is a significant part of the human experience. The issue of sex is important and unavoidable because God, in wisdom and love, chose it to be. Because sex is the creation of God's hand and exists under the control of his sovereignty, we should approach it with reverence and awe, not with embarrassment and timidity. Sex came from him, belongs to him, and continues to exist through him— to him be the glory.

God has also chosen us to live in a world where the lies, deceptions, distortions, and temptations of sex are many. Your address is not a divine mistake. Your exposure to the variegated difficulties of life in this fallen world, with all of its delusions and temptations, is not in the way of God's plan; it *is* his plan. He—right here, right now—has you exactly where he wants you to be. He knows exactly what you're facing. He isn't trying to cope with or cover up a grand divine mistake. He isn't wringing his hands in celestial anxiety. He has carefully and wisely chosen you to live right where you live, knowing full well what you will face. All this is done with divine knowledge and purpose.

So we can't act with regard to sex as if we're powerless, or it will be impossible to prepare for what we will all inevitably face. We can't allow ourselves to think we're alone in the struggle. We can't allow ourselves to live as modern evangelical monastics, as if separation from the world is the key to true righteousness. And we can't be lulled or intimidated into silence in a crucial area of the human existence where the Creator has powerfully and clearly spoken. And we mustn't forget the lie-exposing, freedom-granting truths of the gospel of Jesus Christ. It's vital that we remember that the grace of the Lord Jesus Christ addresses not just our need for past forgiveness or for future hope but also everything we face right here, right now. This gospel is what provides the only reliable diagnostic when it comes to sex, and because it does, the gospel also graces us with the only truly effective cure. The gospel has the power to make us sex-wise, to keep us sex-protected and sex-bold, no longer willing to be sidelined by timidity and fear. The gospel graces us with everything we need to celebrate and participate in human sexuality in a way that honors God and fully enjoys the good things he's given us to enjoy.

Why This Book Now?

People ask me all the time what I am working on or what I intend to write next. They always follow the first question with a second: "Why that now?" And they've surely been intrigued when I've told them I am working on a book about sex. They've been interested in why I've chosen this topic from all the topics I could be addressing, and they ask what I see that motivates me to write about it now. As I've thought about this over the last several months, three words have come to mind again and again, and they are my best answer to the question. The words are *insanity*, *addiction*, and *glory*.

Insanity

Insanity—no, not mine, but the culture's. I'm deeply persuaded that when it comes to sex, we've gone culturally insane. The level of functional delusion, of self-deception and self-destruction, that accompanies the way we approach it is simply crazy. You don't have to look very far to see that we've gone sex insane. We've put sex in a place it was never intended to be, but we seem to fail to see the danger. Our children are sexualized before they're properly educated. I sat in a nice restaurant and was forced to listen to graphic descriptions of sexual "love" that was supposed to be mealtime background music. I had to tear up magazines and put the family computer in a public place in our home to protect my unsuspecting children who were being encouraged to lust before they knew that they were sexual beings. There are few female pop singers able to resist the powerful demands to disrobe and do dance routines that are little more than well-orchestrated simulations of sex. We surely do a better job teaching our girls how to be fashionable than we do teaching them how to be modest and pure. In fact, the words *modest* and *pure* seem strangely weird and antiquated in today's culture. We do a better job of saying no to our children when it comes to what is objectionable than we do teaching them to be good stewards of the desires of their hearts and the functions of their bodies.

Young girls today surely worry more about the beauty of their face and the shape of their body than they do about the quality of their character. Our heroes tend to be people who are young, rich, and sexy rather than heroes in the classic sense of what that word connotes. Young women attach their identity to how thin their nose is, to how full their lips are, and to the size of their breasts. We evaluate one another with terms such as *hot* and *hunk* (they sound more like descriptions of chocolate). Graphic sexual language has become acceptable—and common—in the vocabulary of primetime TV. Pornography is not restricted to the bad neighbors and the dark hallways of rundown buildings. No, it exists on mainstream Internet sites that are a Google click away from anyone with a computer and the most basic computer literacy.

Look around. Listen carefully. Take time to evaluate and consider. Examine the true desires of your own heart. We're in trouble because, in this important place in life, what the human community tends to look at as normal isn't normal at all. It's a web of descending degrees of madness. And in the midst of the madness there's only one window through which we can look at the world of sex and see with candor, clarity, and wisdom. This window is the gospel of the Lord Jesus Christ. And there is only one thing that can free us from the insanity that somehow, someway seems at some point to grip us all. It's the grace of that very same gospel. You see, the humbling truth is that when it comes to sex, we don't have a *thing* problem; the thing (sex) is not evil in itself. We don't have an environment problem, as if our surroundings cause the difficulty. No, we are the problem. The counterintuitive reality is that it's only ever the evil inside us that magnetizes us toward and connects us to the evil that's outside us. Since we are the problem, we really have a problem. We can run from a thing, we can change a relationship, we can move to a different location, but we can't escape ourselves. No, we need rescue, and because we need rescue, we need a rescuer who is wise, powerful, willing, and faithful. That rescuer is the Lord Jesus Christ. He is willing, he is wise, he is able, and he will not forsake us in our time of need.

Addiction

There's a second word that motivated the writing of this book: *addiction*. The dynamic of addiction is that if you look to something that God created to give you what it wasn't intended to give, either you get discouraged quickly and wisely abandon those hopes, or you go back again and again, and in so doing, you begin to travel down addiction's road. That created thing will give you a short-term buzz of euphoria, it will offer you temporary pleasure, it will provide a momentary sense of well-being, it will briefly make you feel that you're something, and it may even make your problems seem not so bad for a bit. It's all very intoxicating. It all feels great. The problem is that the created thing you're looking to has no capacity to satisfy your heart. It wasn't designed to do that. It cannot give you inner peace. It cannot give you the heart rest of contentment. It cannot quiet your cravings. In a word, it cannot be your savior. And if you look outside of the Savior for something to be your savior, that thing will end up being not your savior but your master.

You'll love the short-term buzz, but you'll hate how short it is. So you'll have to go back again quickly to get another shot, and before long you've spent way too much time, energy, and money on something that can't satisfy; but because of what it has briefly done for you each time, you're convinced that you can't live without it. You're hooked, and you may not know it. The thing you once *desired*, you're now persuaded you *need*, and once you've named it as a need, it has you.

Sex is powerfully pleasurable, but it cannot satisfy your heart. The touch of another person stimulates your body and your heart, but it never leaves you fulfilled. Sex connects you in powerful and dramatic ways to another person, but it has no ability whatsoever to make you a better person.

Whether we know it or not, every human being lives in search of a savior. We are all propelled by a quest for identity, inner peace, and some kind of meaning and purpose. And we all look for it somewhere. Here's the bottom line: looking to creation to get what only the Creator can give you always results in addiction of some kind. The thing you hoped would serve you pulls you into its service. What seemed like freedom ends up being bondage. The thing is not the problem; what you've asked of it is.

Glory

This leads to a third word that lies at the foundation of this book. That word is *glory*. As I have written before, human beings are hardwired for glory. That's why we're so attracted to glorious things. We love the glory of a great painting or a beautiful piece of music. We love the excitement of an athletic contest or a feat of daring. We love the sleight of hand of a great magician or the sizzle of a well-seared steak. We love the glory of a moment of success or the recognition of the people around us. We're attracted to the glory of wealth or the beauty of the human body. We're powerfully oriented to glory, and because we are, we live in pursuit of it.

Animals are not like this. Rhinos don't celebrate the size of their horns. Deer don't gather for the biannual long-jump contest. Birds don't envy one another's feathers. Animals don't have this glory orientation, because they weren't made for God in the way that we are. Human beings are hardwired for glory because they are hardwired for God. The glory orientation that's inside every person is meant to drive us to God.

When God created the world, he dyed it with his glory. The created world really is glorious because God made it that way. But the created world is not in possession of *ultimate glory*, the kind of glory that can satisfy your heart. The glory of the created world is *sign* glory. All the glory of the created world is meant to be a sign that points us to the only glory that will ever give rest and peace to our hearts, the glory of God. We were designed to live for that glory. But here's the problem: we lose sight of the fact that the sign isn't the thing. It is there to point us to the thing, and in forgetting this, we ask the sign to do for us what it cannot do.

In this way, life this side of eternity really is one big, unceasing glory battle. There could be no bigger issue than this, than what glory will rule your heart, and in ruling your heart, control your thoughts, desires, choices, words, and behavior. Sinful human beings, in functionally denying the existence of

God, will stop at the sign, won't care about what the sign points them to, and will ask of the sign what it will never be able to give. And that created thing with all its glory will not be their savior; no, it will prove to be a cruel and inglorious master that takes much but gives very little of what they were really seeking. Sex is glorious, but it was created to be a finger that points you to the one glory you were designed to live for—the glory of God.

It's All Vertical

If you've paid attention to our discussion so far, what I'm going to say next shouldn't surprise you. The words *insanity*, *addiction*, and *glory* point us to the fact that our problems with sex will never be solved horizontally. Sex madness is not first a problem of situation, location, or relationship. Sex problems are not first biology or physiology problems. Societal sex addiction doesn't exist because the body is a problem. The fact that we are sexual beings is not the problem. Sex problems are not first the problem of modern media. Sex problems are a matter of the heart. Our problems are deeply spiritual.

The apostle Paul says something striking in 2 Corinthians 5:20. He says that God has called us to be ambassadors of one message—24/7 we mustn't forsake the diagnosis and cure of this solitary message. This message echoes God's unceasing appeal. Here it is: "Be reconciled to God." You see, it's all vertical. The madness that we've briefly considered and that this book will unpack isn't first horizontal, so it won't be fixed horizontally. This insanity is vertical. Only when God is in his rightful place as the unchallenged Master of our hearts will everything else in our lives be in its appropriate place. When something else replaces him, insanity and chaos of some kind always result.

In ways that are formative and practical, we begin to serve the creation as we were designed to serve the Creator, no matter what we say we believe. But it never works; it only leaves us empty, driven, and dissatisfied, the victims of our own bad choices. What we hoped would help us has in fact hooked us. And we cannot run from our problem, because the problem is us. Only when we live practically inside what it means to be reconciled to God will we hold the powerful glories of the created world in the way they were designed to be held.

So continue this journey with me. Either you have sex problems yourself, or you are near to someone who does. You've bought into the insanity, or someone near to you is mad. Look with me at this place of cultural madness through the perfect window of the gospel of Jesus Christ and experience with me the wisdom and freedom that can be found only there.

Review and Reflect

1. Explain why "sex can't deliver the promise that we think it makes, and it's more dangerous than we tend to think" (p. 29).

2. How should we, as Christians, approach discussions about sex? Why do we tend to avoid the topic?

3. Where in your own life have you witnessed the sexual insanity Paul Tripp describes (pp. 32–34)?

4. How do addictions get ahold of the human heart? What does Romans 6:12–23 add to your understanding of addiction?

5. Paul Tripp notes that human beings are "hardwired for glory" (pp. 35–36). What does he mean, and how does it impact our sexuality?

Heart Reset
- 2 Corinthians 5:20

3

The Dangerous Dichotomy

Words are important. They give shape and meaning to things. Much of what you think, desire, know, and choose has been shaped by words. Words have been given special importance to human beings if for no other reason than the fact that God chose to reveal himself in words. We know God for his works (general revelation), but we primarily and specifically know him because of his words (special revelation). If you are a believer, the entire way you think about yourself, life, and the world around you has been shaped by the words of God found on the pages of your Bible. In all things, your calling is to live inside the boundaries of what God has said. But you must begin by understanding the importance, the life-shaping significance, of the first four words of the Bible. You could argue that there are no more important words than these, that everything else the Bible says is built on the foundation of the thunderous implication of these four words. You can't understand yourself, you can't understand life, and you surely can't have a balanced view of the world of sex without understanding the worldview of these four words.

Your Bible begins with these four words: "In the beginning, God" (Gen. 1:1), and with those words everything in life is given its shape, purpose, and meaning. But for the purpose of our topic, these words do something important. They destroy the validity of dividing life into spiritual and secular. This division has opened to us doors of danger as we think about sex. It's allowed us to live with a distance and dissonance between our world of sex and the principles and promises of Scripture. It's caused us to fail to look at this inescapable area of human life from the vantage point of the gospel of Jesus Christ. It's caused us to devalue the practical wisdom of Scripture and to shop for help elsewhere. It's caused us to not avail ourselves of the rescue that can be found only in the person and work of the Lord Jesus Christ. And it's allowed us to minimize the degree to which every sexual act is deeply and inescapably spiritual. The way in which you participate in sex always reveals the true spirituality of your heart.

So I want to take time to unpack the implications of those four words in Genesis 1:1 and apply them to the world of sex. Here's the summary of the implications to follow: *A gospel-centered approach to sex that avoids the insanity of the surrounding culture must begin with looking at life through the window of the doctrine of creation.* The four words that kick off the biblical story of creation, "In the beginning, God," drive us to the following five implications.

1. God exists and is the center of all things.

It is humbling and significant to realize that the biblical story doesn't begin with us. It begins with God. It's important to recognize that the story that unfolds on the pages of your Bible is God's story. He stands on center stage. He has the most important lines. The following spotlight is always on him. The story moves according to his will and by his plan. It's all for him, from him, through him, and about him. He zealously holds on to his position at the center of all things. He will not forsake his position of authority or give his control to another. He is the center, the important one, and the Lord of glory. Your understanding of everything in your life must begin here.

Your life is not about you; it is about him. It's vital to know that you were born into a universe that by its very nature is a celebration of him. It's only when he is in his proper place in your heart, that is, at the center, that everything else in your life will be in its appropriate place and balance. What this means practically is that everything exists for his pleasure and glory and not for yours. So you and I must approach everything in a way that gives God the glory that belongs to him. If you forget him and his glory, you'll use things for no higher purpose than your own glory, and in so doing you'll misuse them in some way. Again, the recognition of God's centrality in all things, and the existence of all things for his glory, is not so much about being superspiritual. It's about recapturing the full meaning of your humanity. This is the way all human beings were made to live. To insert yourself into the center of your world is to violate the very nature of the world, and that isn't the fundamental way that all things were designed to operate. To violate basic creation order and design never goes anywhere good, no matter what dimension of our lives we're talking about.

Practical, everyday "me-ism," where the world is reduced to the small confines of your comfort, your pleasure, your control, your happiness, and your ease, never works. It doesn't work because it runs cross-grain against the way you and the world you live in were meant to operate. You see, it's simply not about you, and when you make it about you, nothing good results. God-forgetting self-sovereignty is dangerous to you and destructive to your heart and will cause you to use things in a way they were not intended to be used. Because of this, "me-ism" never results in long-term peace, rest, satisfaction, and joy.

When you put yourself and your particular definition of pleasure at the center of your world, not only are you rejecting God's wisdom and rebelling against his authority, but you're also questing for his position. But God, in his zeal for his own glory and for your good, won't exit his position and give it to you. You just can't properly understand and participate in the world of sex without this perspective. Think about this.

Our problem with sex doesn't begin with lust, with bad choices, or with sexual misbehavior. Our problem with sex begins when we forget that God must be at the center of this part of our lives as he must be with any other. When you have no greater motivation in sex than your own satisfaction, you are already in sexual trouble, even if you don't know it yet. *How have you tended to put yourself in the center of your world of sexuality?*

Whether or not you functionally recognize it, at the epicenter of your sexual world exists a God of awesome power, glory, and grace. Sex in its rightful place in your heart and life always begins by recognizing that he is at the center.

2. God is the creator and owner of all that exists.

My words here, "God is the creator and owner of all that exists," have been chosen carefully. You cannot have the first word (creator) without the other (owner). The concept of creation always carries with it the resulting concepts of design and ownership. Perhaps two of the most important questions you could ask about anything in your life are, What was the

Creator's purpose for this thing when it was made? And, What does it look like for me to recognize the Creator's ownership over this thing as I use it in my daily living? Because you and I are creatures and not the Creator, it isn't our prerogative to relate to our lives and the things in our lives as if we are the owners and designers. When you act as though every function of your body belongs to you, you're forgetting the Creator and heading for trouble.

Here's what's important to understand: human beings were designed to be resident managers of the created world that God owns. God made and owned the beautiful garden of Eden, placed Adam and Eve in it, and then commissioned them to live in and care for the garden he made and owned. They didn't own what they'd been given. They didn't make the rules. They didn't get a vote when it came to the purpose for their own lives and for everything else. They were there to recognize God's ownership by fulfilling his purpose.

I find these perspectives to be very convicting. When I'm thinking about physical intimacy with Luella, am I conscious at that moment that my body and my sexuality belong to the Lord? Let's be honest—it's counterintuitive to think this way. It's natural to be propelled by sexual desire, forgetting that there is One who owns every aspect of our sexuality.

I'm afraid that we don't think in helpful ways in these areas because we've reduced our relationship with sex to a set of rules. But God's rules aren't arbitrary. They're not just a set of disconnected moral abstractions. They don't make any sense when viewed or presented that way. God's rules are rooted in relationship. It is here alone that they get their rationality and beauty. You see, we were designed for relationship with God, a relationship in which we would daily recognize his position as our Creator and our position as his creatures. All of God's rules are an outgrowth, an expression of, or an application of the thing for which we were made—relationship with him. This relationship was to be shaped by worshipful love and joyful obedience. Celebrating God's existence, wisdom, power, and glory means that we have no complaint about staying inside his boundaries.

This means that you cannot have a sensible discussion of the sexual dysfunction of human culture by just discussing the evidences of its sexual insanity. You can recognize and critique dysfunction only when you're examining it from the perspective of ownership, purpose, and design. Any principle you would apply to sex, as wise as it may be, makes sense only in the face of the reality that there was a purpose for all of creation that resided in the mind of the Creator. To know God's mind is to know his purpose, and to know his purpose is to understand how sex is meant to be used, and to know how sex is meant to be used allows you to then recognize and critique its misuse.

One other thing needs to be emphasized here. It's important to understand that *ownership* living, where you live as if your life and everything in it belongs to you, never results in the lasting rest, joy, peace, happiness, and fulfillment that every human being seeks. We need only the shocking and sad story of the disobedience in the garden to tell us where ownership living leads. You cannot have the peace of heart that's the quest of everyone and violate the core principle of the universe, that is, the centrality of God in all things.

3. Because God is a spirit, and we are made in his image and for relationship with him, all of life is spiritual.

Human beings tend to make sense out of life by dividing it into meaningful categories. Political, work, economic, education, gender, social, familial, age, and entertainment categories function as a conceptual tool kit for us. You hear the category, and you know in some general way what you're dealing with. This is all well and good as long as your order-giving categories are good ones. Bad categories can lead to sloppy, nonsensical thinking but more importantly to bad living. I'm afraid that this is what's happened with the age-old categories of *spiritual* and *secular*. You cannot take the first four words of the Bible seriously and be comfortable with dividing your world into the secular and the spiritual. Now, I know there are endeavors in life that are self-consciously religious, and there are activities that are decidedly not. But that isn't what we're talking about here. We're talking about dividing your life into things that have to do with God and things that don't or, even more dangerously, things in life that belong to God and things that belong to you. So God gets the religious, devotional, churchistic part of your existence, and everything else is secular—that is, not necessarily connected to the spiritual part of your life—as long as in those areas you keep the Ten Commandments.

The first four words of the Bible immediately alert you to the fact that you cannot divide life this way. It cannot be sectored into the spiritual and the secular: God and mine, religious and non-religious, faith and facts, or whatever other categories you would use to separate things that are Godward and those that are not. You end up with a dangerous schizophrenia of heart that creates havoc at the street level. Since all of life was made by God, it exists through him, is there for him, and is designed to operate according to his plan. There is no purely secular domain of your life. Your very existence as a human being made in God's image connects you to him all the time. Everywhere you go and in everything you do, you encounter things that were made by him, connecting you to him once again. He reveals himself in powerful ways in his creation. God is inescapable. He is literally the environment in which you live. As I have said many, many times, you can't get up in the morning without bumping into God.

So sex is not an a-religious thing. Sex is deeply spiritual. Your relationship to your own sexuality and the sexuality of others always reveals your heart. Your sexual life is always an expression of what you truly worship. Sex is deeply religious. In sex you are either self-consciously submitting to God or setting yourself up as God. In other words, sex is never simply a horizontal thing. Sex always connects you to the God who created your body, gave you eyes to see and a heart that desires, and tells you how you are to steward this aspect of your personhood.

I'm afraid that there's more of this *spiritual versus secular* dichotomy hanging around in our thinking and the way we approach life than we may think. And when we've divided our world this way, we've little defense against the insanity of the surrounding culture. We see this clearly in an example I gave in the last chapter—the way in which most Christian parents talk to their children about sex. They tend to have a single talk about how the bodies of men and women are made and how they sexually function, and then they give their children a set of do's and don'ts. Such an approach simply doesn't prepare young people to defend themselves against the constant stream of sexual insanity that they'll be exposed to almost everywhere they look. These parents mean well, but they've not rooted the whole topic of sexuality in the reality of the existence of God, in the glory of his love, wisdom, power, and grace and in the peace, fulfillment, and security of living the way we were designed to live—for him. Armed with little more than an "I'm not supposed to" approach to sexuality, their children have little protection from the seductive voices that will constantly whisper in their ears.

It's only an "everything is spiritual because everything is worship" view of life that builds for us a defense against the insanity that's both inside and outside us.

4. Since God is the creator and controller of all things, he alone is worthy of our worship.

I've said it already, but I want to expand on what it means here. Your sexual world *is* a world of worship. Now, I'm sure, for many readers, this needs explanation. For many of us, *worship* is a tricky word. We tend to think of worship in restricted, formal worship ways. But it's important to understand that worship is your identity as a human being. You were designed for worship. This means that you're always attaching the hopes, dreams, peace, motivations, joy, and security of your heart to something. So you don't worship just on Sunday; you worship your way through every day of your life. A worshiper is who you are; worship is what you do. So sex is an act of worship in some way. When you think of worship, don't think just of a weekend religious activity; think of a lifestyle. Let me explain further.

Scripture lays out four aspects of the lifestyle of worship. First, to worship means to *bow down*. This is the devotional, affective part of worship. The posture connoted by these words is important. In bowing down, I kneel before God and offer him the affections of my heart. I give him the honor he is due. I bring to him the deepest of offerings, the love of my heart. I bow to his majesty, his authority, his centrality, and his holiness. I recognize that he exists and that I was made by and for him. Remember that as you use sex, you're always bowing down to someone or something. You cannot escape the "bowing down" aspect of this significant area of your life.

Second, to worship means to *obey*. Here I recognize God's wisdom and his rule. In obedience I am stating that I know my life doesn't belong to me, that I wasn't created to write my own rules. Obedience is worship at the most mundane of levels. Here I'm submitting the detailed choices and actions of my life to God's greater wisdom and authority. So in sex you are either worshiping God by willingly submitting to his wise and good rules or writing your own rules, and in so doing, telling yourself that you're smarter than God.

Also, to worship means to *trust*. To trust means to willingly place your life, your welfare, your future, and your inner sense of well-being in God's hands. It's not only to assent to the fact that he is good and his way is always right but also to think, desire, speak, and act as though you really do. Your sexual activity always expresses trust in someone or something.

Finally, to worship means to *serve*. Here I submit the agenda, the hopes and dreams, or the plan of my life to the greater plans of God. In worship I walk away from my little self-satisfied kingdom of one where I reign as a self-appointed sovereign, and I give the time, energy, and resources of my life to the plans, purposes, and work of the kingdom of God. It's inescapably true that you always have sex in service of one of these two kingdoms. In sex you will remember that God didn't give you his grace to make your little kingdom successful but to welcome you to a much bigger and much better kingdom.

Your sexual world is a world of worship. The big question is not, "Are you in or out of trouble?" but, "In sex, what in the world are you worshiping?"

5. The purpose of the cross is to reconcile us to God and restore God to his rightful place in our hearts.

The first four words of the Bible explain to us the rest of the story of the Bible. It's only in the face of the reality that we were made for God and that everything exists for him that the necessity of Jesus's coming and the cross make sense. Since sin separates us from God and causes us to live for ourselves, and since there's nothing we can do to earn our way back into God's favor, a savior had to come. The Savior would have to live the life we should have lived and die the death that was our due and rise again, defeating sin and death. All this was necessary so that we would not only be guaranteed eternal life but also be reconciled to God.

You see, it's only when we're in right relationship with God, when we're living for him and not for ourselves, when we're entrusting ourselves to his good purpose and following his wise rule, that everything in our lives is in its proper place. Hope for sexual sanity is found only in one place: at the foot of the cross of the Lord Jesus Christ. Sanity in this area will never be found in trying harder and doing better, because it's what lives inside rather than outside of you that you most need to defend yourself against. It's humbling but vital to admit that the greatest sex dangers are those you carry around inside you, and you take them with you wherever you go and to whomever you're with.

So the first four words of the Bible, "In the beginning, God," drive me to one conclusion: I need a savior of glorious and transforming grace, because I need to be saved from me. Without the grace of this Savior, I'll join the company of the insane and use my body in ways it was never meant to be used. But there's hope for me, because this Savior has come, and he's poured out his grace. He gives me much more than a set of rules; he gives me himself. Not only does he forgive me, but he comes and lives inside me and, in so doing, begins to transform me at the causal core of my personhood, my heart. By grace he daily fights on my behalf. By grace he causes me to love wisdom and to hate foolishness. By grace he leads me to love his kingdom more than I love my own. By grace he convicts me when I'm wrong and restores me with his forgiveness. By grace he invites me to run to him and not from him when I've failed to measure up. And someday by grace he'll take me to a place where the insanity is no more.

If all of life is spiritual, then the deepest sex need of every human being who's ever taken a breath is a Savior. He has come. There is hope!

Review and Reflect

1. What happens when we divide our world into two distinct categories, sacred and secular? Why do we know that such a division is actually unnatural?

2. Why does a self-centered lifestyle breed misery rather than happiness?

3. How does acknowledging God's ownership of everything in creation—including our bodies—foster sexual sanity?

4. Explain what Paul Tripp means when he writes, "Your sexual world is a world of worship" (p. 49). Scripture lays out four aspects of a worshiping lifestyle. How has each aspect shaped your sex life?

5. How do the first four words of the Bible, "In the beginning, God" (Gen. 1:1), drive us to see our need of a Savior?

Heart Reset

- Genesis 1:1

- Proverbs 8:22–36

4

So Why Do We Do the Things We Do?

He was in trouble long before he knew it. As he assessed his life, he concluded that he was okay, but he wasn't. He saw himself as a mature Christian, a committed family man, and a diligent worker. But he was running toward disaster without any sense of concern or fear.

He had worked with her for years. They were on a management team and often in meetings together. For almost a decade their relationship had been strictly business, that is, until that day she asked if she could share a table with him in the executive dining room. That morning had been ridiculously stressful. His children had been out of control, and he and his wife were not in a very good place. When he left for work, everybody was mad at everybody, and his goodbye gesture to his wife was a dirty look rather than the usual perfunctory kiss.

He must have had the posture and facial expression of a beaten man, because when she sat down with her lunch tray, her opening line was not about business; it was about him. "You look like you've been hit by a Mack truck," she said, half jokingly.

"You have no idea," he responded.

"Oh, yeah?" she replied.

"It's not work," he said. "Things are great here; it's home. Sometimes it all just seems impossible. Too many complicated relationships with too many people all at once. It's all I can do to turn off the stress before I get here so I can concentrate on the job and not get myself fired," he moaned.

"If you're anything at home like you are here, you must be a pretty good husband and father. I'm sure your family is blessed to have you around," she said as she looked at her watch, excused herself, and rushed out of the room.

He watched her leave, thinking, "That was really nice; the most encouragement I've gotten in months." He went back to work and his busy life and didn't think about her for days until they had their first semimonthly executive meeting. He noticed her in ways he hadn't before. She got his attention in ways that the other participants hadn't. He tried not to look at her because he didn't want to make her uncomfortable, but he kept looking at her. After the meeting he went back to his overloaded desk. He tried to deny it, but he was glad when, a couple days later, she came into his office to ask him a few departmental questions. Before she left, she asked, "Are things less stressful at home?" He smiled and rolled his eyes as she exited his office. He sat, watching her go, completely unaware that something dramatic and important, potentially life changing, was happening in his heart. He still thought he was okay.

In the kind of denial that seems to accompany these temptations, he told himself that nothing had changed, but it had. He began to come to work hoping he would see her. No, he didn't want a relationship with her, and, no, he'd entertained no thoughts whatsoever of sex, but in his heart their relationship had definitely changed. He didn't often eat in the lunchroom, but he began to regularly. He told himself that it was good for the department, but that's not why he was there. He was there in the hope that she would be there. She often was, and their having lunch together began to happen more frequently.

With each lunch his affection compass was pointed increasingly in her direction. He hadn't abandoned his commitment to his wife, and he surely hadn't entertained any thoughts of leaving his marriage, but his heart had moved, and because it had, it wouldn't be long before his body moved as well. He told himself that she was just another colleague, but she wasn't. He told himself that it was important to develop solid friendships with fellow workers, but he seemed to have that bond only with her. Their conversations became more frequent, more planned, and more personal, but he still had no sense of danger.

One time in the hallway, they were laughing about something, and she touched his hand. He felt a buzz at that moment that he had only ever felt with his wife. She had touched him, and he liked it. He wanted her to touch him again. No, he wasn't thinking of sex, but he liked her, and he liked being close to her. He liked the thought of being physically close. The heart that he should have protected long before was now no longer searching or attracted; it was hooked. But he simply didn't recognize how hooked he was.

His wife grew concerned. It wasn't because he was staying late at work; he wasn't. It wasn't that she had found an unexplained receipt or something on his cell phone. No, she noticed differences in the way he related to her. He seemed distant and even less communicative. He was surely more impatient and irritable than usual. He had quit giving her that perfunctory kiss. And it had been a long time since he had shown any interest in having sex with her. She had approached him several times with her concern, and he had blamed it on burdens from work, claiming he would try to do better at leaving those burdens at the door. But nothing changed. She was worried, but she didn't know what to worry about.

Meanwhile his relationship with his female colleague had gotten quite physical. I don't mean *physical* in an overtly sexual sense. I mean that their relationship had become quite tactile. He would put his arm around her when he asked how she was doing. She would stand with her body actually touching him as they waited in the hallway for a meeting. He would grab her hand when he was making a point or touch her shoe with his shoe under the table in a meeting. All this appeared to him and maybe to others as harmless, but it wasn't harmless at all. It wasn't harmless because all of it was sexual, highly sexual. He had weeks earlier committed adultery in his heart; that is, he had shifted the affection of his heart from his wife to his fellow worker, and now he was beginning to commit adultery with his body. It was all office-acceptable foreplay, and it wouldn't be long before sex would follow.

It was in the stairwell of the parking garage as they were both leaving for the day that she reached up and gave him a kiss on the cheek as she said goodbye. He looked around to see if anyone was near and responded with a kiss on her lips. Embarrassed, they both rushed away, but it wouldn't be long before they rented a hotel room for the disaster they'd been heading toward for a very long time.

He sat with me, now estranged from his wife and having left his well-paying job, depressed, self-righteous, and confused. "She knew I was married, and she set me up anyway," he said defensively. It was the same old self-righteous, self-atoning delusion I'd heard many times before. He'd thrown away a wonderful marriage to a good lady and his relationship to three beautiful children for twenty minutes of sexual pleasure. He knew what he'd done was wrong, but he still held on to the possibility that he wasn't to blame. Adulterous, yet innocent—how does that happen?

So Why Do We Do the Things We Do?

It was a dramatic, game-changing moment. It's recorded for us in Matthew 5:27–30. Jesus is unfolding the gospel principles of his kingdom. I've often wondered about the reaction of the crowd as he spoke these words:

> You have heard that it was said, "You shall not commit adultery." But I say to you that everyone who looks at a woman with lustful intent has already committed adultery with her in his heart. If your right eye causes you to sin, tear it out and throw it away. For it is better that you lose one of your members than that your whole body be thrown into hell. And if your right hand causes you to sin, cut it off and throw it away. For it is better that you lose one of your members than that your whole body go into hell.

In these words not only does Christ lay out the original intent of God's law and define where the real moral battle is raging, but he also drops a bomb on any hope that legalism can produce righteous living. Let me give you the helicopter view of this little passage and then draw out some of its implications for our topic.

These words are humbling to hear but vitally important to consider because Christ is saying something counterintuitive to the way most of us think about ourselves and try to make sense out of our lives. From fifty thousand feet, what Christ is doing here in the area of sex is answering the question that every human being asks at some time: Why do people do the things they do? And related to that, why do we say the things we say and make the decisions we make? Why do we successfully fight some things and willfully give in to others? Why do we tell ourselves that we won't do certain things but end up doing them anyway? Why?

The war of sex is never just a battle with the temptations of the surrounding culture; it is never just about behavior or about what we do with our bodies. Christ is saying that our behavior is directed more by what's inside us than the people and situations outside us. He's saying that sexual struggles are inescapably struggles of the heart. Physical adultery is simply the body going where the heart has gone long ago. And as Christ says this, he gives thoughts and desires the moral value of actions. You don't cross the adultery boundary only when you have illicit sex. You cross the boundary when you give your heart to thoughts and desires that are outside God's will for you. You will never win the battle with sexual sin by just attempting to harness your behavior, because every wrong sexual act is connected to a decision, which is connected to a desire in your heart. You always give your heart away before you surrender your body to what is wrong.

Listen to the hard-to-hear words of Mark 7:20–23:

> And he said, "What comes out of a person is what defiles him. For from within, out of the heart of man, come evil thoughts, sexual immorality, theft, murder, adultery, coveting, wickedness, deceit, sensuality, envy, slander, pride, foolishness. All these evil things come from within, and they defile a person."

Notice that Jesus doesn't say, "Hey guys, it's very simple. The problem is, you live in this broken and evil world that isn't functioning as I intended. It's populated with sinful people who seduce you into doing what's wrong. So if you want to live a godly life, you have to determine to separate yourself from both." But that's how we tend to think. I've heard adulterous husbands say to me, "Paul, if you lived with my wife, you would understand why I did what I did." I've heard adulterous women blame the seductive power of their lover. I've heard parents of a pregnant teenager blame TV, YouTube, and Facebook. I've heard pastors who've committed sexual sin point to the lonely burdens of stressful ministry. Again and again I hear people instinctively pointing outside themselves to answer the question *Why did I do what I did?* But listen to the words of Jesus and let them sink in: "What comes out of a person is what defiles him."

Here's where the words of Christ drive us: our struggle with sexual sin is not first a struggle with the environment in which we live or with the people that we live near. Our struggle with sexual sin reveals the dark and needy condition of our hearts. We are our biggest problem. When it comes to sexual sin, the greatest sexual danger to any human being anywhere lives inside him, not outside. Isolation, changes of location and relationship, and management of behavior never work because they don't target the place where the problem exists—the heart. Sexual struggles have a much deeper beginning point than your eyes and your sexual organs.

So if sexual problems arise from the heart, it's important to make some biblical observations about the heart. I'm persuaded that you can't have a real, life-changing conversation about sexual insanity without these heart principles from Scripture.

1. You need to know what the Bible is talking about when it talks about the heart.

Scripture presents the heart as the seat of our emotion, motivation, will, thought, and desire. This means that when you encounter the word *heart* in your Bible, you should have the following definition in your brain: the heart is the *causal center of your personhood.* People do what they do because of what's in their heart. Situations don't cause you to do what you do. People don't cause you to do what you do. Locations don't cause you to do what you do. Your heart does. That's the Bible's humbling bottom line.

2. You need to understand that the heart is always functioning under the rule of something.

The heart is a control center. Your heart is always submitting to the rulership of something. And there are only two possibilities. Your heart functions under the control of the Creator or the creation. Now, grasping this is more helpful than it may at first seem. It isn't wrong to desire pleasure, but if you love pleasure more than you love God, you're heading for trouble. It isn't wrong to enjoy comfort, but if your heart is more controlled by desire for comfort than by love for God, you're heading somewhere not good. You see, the problem is not that your heart has the capacity to desire; the problem is ruling desire. Let me say it as I've said it before: *the desire for even a good thing becomes a bad thing when that desire becomes a ruling thing.* When the pleasures of sex exercise more control over your heart than the will of God does, your heart has already stepped beyond God's boundaries, and your body will soon follow.

3. You need to realize that what controls your heart will direct your behavior.

Your behavior is inextricably connected to the thoughts and desires of your heart. People and situations may be the occasion and location of what you do, but never the cause. So when you have done with sex what God says you should not do, you can't look outside yourself for explanations. You must look inside. If, as Jesus says, you've already committed adultery in your heart, it won't be long before you commit the act with the members of your body. Here's what these two diagnostic passages tell us: it is always the sin of thought and desire in your heart that hooks you to the evil in the world in which you live. Your problem when it comes to sex is much deeper than an entertainment and media culture that has simply gone crazy. Your problem is the self-oriented, pleasure-addicted insanity that lives inside you and makes you an easy target for the madness of the society around you. Monasteries and boycotts simply don't create pure living; never have, never will.

4. You need to realize that this side of eternity, your heart is susceptible.

Because our heart leaves us vulnerable, we must humbly admit that we live in a constant state of susceptibility. None of us has a pure heart. You read it right—not one of us. Yes, by the grace of the cross, the power of sin has been broken, but that doesn't mean we are sin-free. No, sin still lives with deceptive and destructive power in each one of our hearts, even though its hold is being progressively eradicated by God's sanctifying grace. I'd like to think that I am one of the pure ones, but I give regular empirical evidence that I'm not. We all carry impure desires inside us. We all think impure thoughts. We all dream impure dreams. We all crave what we shouldn't crave. All of us. This side of heaven, complete moral purity is a self-righteous delusion that we would all do well to reject. Our hearts continue to be dark and messy as grace continues to work to purify us.

You are susceptible every moment of your life because, admit it, there are still areas where you want what you should not want. In silence, secrecy, or a lack of self-knowledge, you look at things in a way that you should not look, you begin to consider what you should not consider, and you entertain dreams you should not entertain. You're in the process of offering up your susceptible heart, all the while telling yourself that you are pure.

5. You need to admit that this side of eternity, your heart is fickle.

I get uncomfortable in those worship-service moments when we sing, "You are my all in all," "You're my priceless treasure," "With all my heart I love you," or "I adore you." I often stop singing and think, "Really? Do I?" Does love for God rule my heart unchallenged? Does it? Is God at the center of my affections, the focus of my greatest joys? Really, is he? I think we seriously underestimate the fickle nature of our sinful hearts. We quickly switch loyalties. We rapidly trade affection for one thing for another. We all too easily give way to our love. We willingly abandon commitments we forcefully made. We fail to do what we promised. We abandon our dreams for what we think would be a better dream. Our hearts will only ever be truly loyal and stable when our hearts are sin-free. As long as sin lives inside us in some way, we're all sadly shopping for a better, more satisfying master, denying the glory of the Master whom by grace we've been given.

6. You need to face the fact that this side of eternity, your heart is deceptive.

We would all like to think that no one knows our heart better than we do. We would like to believe that others may be self-deceived, but we are not. It's simply not true. Since sin is in its essence deceptive, as long as sin lives in our hearts, we will tend to be blind to the true condition of our hearts. But more must be said. Not only will we be blind to our hearts; we will be blind to our blindness, thinking we see when we really don't. To add to this, we will participate in our own blindness. Because of the self-righteousness of sin, we will work to make ourselves feel good about what is not good or to believe that the problem is not, in fact, us. So the man who has looked too long at a woman at work in a way he should not will tell himself that it is not lust, that he's just one of those guys who notices the beauty of God's creation. ("Is it a sin to recognize when a woman is beautiful?") A relationship that has grown emotional and a bit physical will be characterized as a close friendship. ("Is it wrong to have close female friends?") A woman who has begun to replace her husband emotionally will say she needs friendships with other men. ("Is it wrong for a married woman to hear the perspectives of another man?") Each question is self-atoning. Each person is a participant in the deception of his or her own heart. Since the heart is deceptive, we are often in sexual danger long before our eyes see it and our heart admits it.

7. You need to face the fact that your body will wander where your heart has already gone.
I don't need to say much more about this; I've said much already. I think, though, that this point needs to be highlighted: sexual problems are symptomatic of deeper problems of the heart, and if you give away your heart, you simply will not be successful in controlling your body.

8. You need to confess that your behavior always reveals more about you than about your situation, location, or relationships.
It is here, I think, that the evangelical church has tended to lack honesty, integrity, and biblical accuracy. When it comes to the growing sexual insanity that exists in our churches (Internet pornography, marital adultery, and singles having sex), we have tended to point our fingers in the wrong direction. We have talked much about the shocking sexual degradation and coarseness of the surrounding culture. And it is shocking. We talk about the sexual images from which it is almost impossible to protect our children. We point to the sexualization of the fashion and entertainment industries. And we should talk about those things. We

talk about how the Internet has been morally kidnapped by a global, multibillion-dollar pornography empire. We talk about the moral insanity of high school health classes. We talk about how sexual humor infects even the family sitcom. All these things are issues and need discussion and action, but self-delusion and self-righteousness make the conversation hard and set us up for greater difficulty.

The sexual madness that lives in the seats of our Sunday services exposes and indicts the true condition of our hearts. The debt and materialism that live in our congregations reveal more about us than about the surrounding culture. Here's what's important about this chapter: when you tell yourself that the problem is not you, when you deny the centrality of your heart in every choice and action you make, and when you minimize the dangerous impurity that still lives inside you, you don't seek the help you desperately need, and you don't set up the protections that are clearly called for. As a result, you set yourself up to be seduced and deceived once again.

So What Now?

Well, we must all face the fact that changes in our personal sex life don't begin with cultural analysis; they begin with personal confession. Change doesn't begin with pointing to the difficulty of your situation or to the behavior of the people around you. Change begins in one place: with heart-deep confession. When it comes to sex, we all need to say that the biggest problem in our sexual lives is us.

I would challenge you to pray with me David's prayer of humble confession (Psalm 51). Do it right here, right now.

> Have mercy on me, O God,
>   according to your steadfast love;

according to your abundant mercy
  blot out my transgressions.
Wash me thoroughly from my iniquity,
  and cleanse me from my sin!

For I know my transgressions,
  and my sin is ever before me.
Against you, you only, have I sinned
  and done what is evil in your sight,
so that you may be justified in your words
  and blameless in your judgment.
Behold, I was brought forth in iniquity,
  and in sin did my mother conceive me.
Behold, you delight in truth in the inward being,
  and you teach me wisdom in the secret heart.

Purge me with hyssop, and I shall be clean;
  wash me, and I shall be whiter than snow.
Let me hear joy and gladness;
  let the bones that you have broken rejoice.
Hide your face from my sins,
  and blot out all my iniquities.
Create in me a clean heart, O God,
  and renew a right spirit within me.
Cast me not away from your presence,
  and take not your Holy Spirit from me.
Restore to me the joy of your salvation,
  and uphold me with a willing spirit.

Then I will teach transgressors your ways,
  and sinners will return to you.
Deliver me from bloodguiltiness, O God,
    O God of my salvation,
  and my tongue will sing aloud of your righteousness.
O Lord, open my lips,
  and my mouth will declare your praise.

> For you will not delight in sacrifice, or I would give it;
>> you will not be pleased with a burnt offering.
> The sacrifices of God are a broken spirit;
>> a broken and contrite heart, O God, you will not despise.
>
> Do good to Zion in your good pleasure;
>> build up the walls of Jerusalem;
> then will you delight in right sacrifices,
>> in burnt offerings and whole burnt offerings;
>> then bulls will be offered on your altar.

You see, if our sex problems are a matter of our hearts, if it is true that we do what we do because of what's in our hearts, then we need something more than cultural analysis, biblical information, and rules. Give a man who is addicted to Internet pornography a set of rules and see how far that takes him. Sexual sin is a matter of the heart. Our only hope for personal purity and for a defense against cultural insanity is found in the transformation of our hearts, and for that we need the very same mercy for which David cries out in this beautiful, heart-wrenching psalm.

Won't you stop right now and cry out for the very same grace? You need it right now as much as David did, whether or not you admit that to yourself.

Review and Reflect

1. Reread Jesus's words in Matthew 5:27–30. What was Jesus teaching here, and how is the lesson reinforced in Mark 7:20–23?

2. What turns a good desire into something bad? Where have you seen this happen in your own life? Trace the particular ways in which this desire of yours went from good to bad.

3. Paul Tripp writes, "Monasteries and boycotts simply don't create pure living" (p. 61). Explain what he means.

4. Why is humility necessary to accurately understand how our heart functions? How does a right understanding keep us sexually sane?

5. As you examine your life and heart, where do you see a need for change? How does such change begin? Form your answer from specific portions of Psalm 51.

Heart Reset

- Matthew 5:27–30

- Mark 7:20–23

- Psalm 51

5

The Highest Pleasure

The multilayered beauty of a sunset.

The sweet song of a bird.

The biting herbaceousness of cilantro.

The tender delicacy of a human kiss.

The whistle of the breeze through leaves of a giant oak.

The cacophony of sound that is the animal kingdom.

The shimmer of a glassy, still pond.

The variegated beauty of the human form.

The gorgeous aroma of a rose.

The seemingly endless catalog of herbs and spices.

The emotional power of music.

The communicative power of visual art.

The gift of eyes, ears, mouth, nose, and hands to take it all in.

The existence of the desire for pleasure.

The ability to recognize and enjoy beauty.

The capacity to create beauty.

The endless sights, sounds, shapes, colors, light, and textures of the created world.

The sedentary pleasure of sleep.

The fact that all this and more is available to us every day.

The pleasures of life are everywhere you turn. They greet you every day and all throughout the day. You couldn't escape pleasure if you tried. Do you know why? There is only one answer: because God wanted it that way. With wisdom and purpose, he created a world stuffed to overflowing with pleasures of every kind. There are pleasures of sight, sound, taste, and touch. There are pleasures of thought and emotion. There are pleasures of location, situation, and relationship. Pleasure exists because it fits with God's purpose for his creation. It is one of his chief gifts to us. But you and I need to understand the role of pleasure in God's creation and how we are to respond to the pleasures that greet us every day.

Let me start by noting this: you simply cannot write a book about sex and avoid the larger topic of pleasure. Maybe the best way to say it is this: if you get pleasure wrong, you tend to misuse sex. So before we begin to look at sex more specifically and in much greater detail, it is vital that we address the core issue—pleasure.

The Birth of Pleasure

It is not an overstatement of a distant theological platitude to say that pleasure and its birth are in the mind of God. Legitimate pleasure of any type is God's creation, and our ability to recognize and enjoy pleasure is the result of his design. There is no better place to see this and to trace its implications than to go back to the beginning, to the garden of Eden. I want to introduce you to the *Eden hermeneutic*. Hermeneutics is the science of interpretation. You and I live life based not on the facts of our existence but on our unique and personal interpretation of the facts. Here's how it works for our topic: if God created pleasure, then pleasure is not the problem. The problem comes when we understand pleasure in the wrong way and then involve ourselves in pleasure in ways that directly result from the wrong interpretations we have made.

So like everything else, when it comes to pleasure, we need some kind of interpretive guide, and God's creation of the garden of Eden and the placing of Adam and Eve in it provide the perfect interpretive tool for us. Let me suggest five critical perspectives on pleasure that emerge as we look at it through the interpretive window of the garden.

1. The ascetics have it wrong.

Asceticism (from the Greek word for "training" or "exercise") has been around for a long time and still exists in various forms in evangelical Christianity. The chief worldview of the ascetic is that by renouncing worldly pleasures, one can achieve a higher spiritual state. The problem with asceticism is that it misunderstands the nature of God's creation and of human beings and, in so doing, makes pleasure the problem. The existence of the garden of Eden in a world of perfection simply blows asceticism away.

God didn't cruelly place Adam and Eve in an environment of dangerous and evil pleasure and then require them to avoid it in fear of their destruction and his judgment. He didn't require abstinence as a true test of the loyalty and godliness of their hearts; the opposite is true. He placed them in an environment of delicious pleasures and set them free to enjoy. The garden was full of the pleasures of sight, sound, smell, touch, and taste. The garden introduced them to the pleasures of emotional and sexual love. It was a gloriously pleasurable place to live, and there was simply nothing inherently evil or dangerous in any of it. Being what God created Adam and Eve to be did not demand avoidance; it required participation. Asceticism is wrong because it curses creation and assesses holiness by the degree of one's separation from creation. This doesn't put God in his rightful place.

It does just the opposite. It views him as either cruel or unwise or both. It presents him not as one you want to run to but as one to protect yourself from.

Asceticism also misunderstands the nature of human beings. It gets to the heart of what I have given myself to write about. Human beings are inside-out beings. That is, we do what we do not so much because of what is outside us but because of what is inside us. If God had created people whose choices and behavior were hopelessly determined by what lies outside, he surely wouldn't have placed them in an environment of such gorgeous delights. They would have been quickly overwhelmed and soon addicted, unable to control themselves because of the powerful determinants everywhere around them.

Adam and Eve weren't made like that. They were given hearts that could think, imagine, consider, weigh, choose, feel, regret, and worship. And God knew that as long as their hearts were not controlled by pleasure but ruled by him, they would be able to engage in pleasure in a God-glorifying way and not lose their way.

The creation of the garden of delights and the tragedy of the rebellion of Genesis 3 come together to tell us this one vital thing: pleasure isn't your problem; you are. It sounds unkind, doesn't it? But it's true. It bears repeating that all pleasure problems are heart problems. We haven't gone sex insane because sex exists. Rather, our sex insanity reveals the disloyalty and rebellion of our hearts. So we don't deal with sex problems by naming sex as something evil to be avoided. It is not worldly to really enjoy sex (in its God-ordained context). Celibate people aren't spiritual nobility.

The garden says it all. Separating yourself from the very pleasures that point to God's glory and were given to you to enjoy doesn't solve the pleasure problem. Rather, it blames the pleasureable thing and calls into question the wisdom and love of the One who created it.

2. Pleasure is God-glorifying.

God's creative intention was to bring glory to himself by the pleasures he created. Each pleasurable thing was perfectly created and designed to reflect and point to the greater glory of the One who created it. These things were designed to be pleasure inducing but also for a deeply spiritual purpose. They were meant to remind you of him. They were meant to amaze you not just with their existence but with the wisdom, power, and glory of the One who made them. They were put on earth to be one of God's means of getting your attention and capturing your heart.

You see, you will never understand pleasure if you think it is an end in itself. Pleasure is pleasurable, and you should never feel guilty for enjoying it or for wanting more. Your enjoyment of pleasure is all according to God's design. But you and I must understand that pleasure has a purpose beyond the momentary enjoyment it gives us. Pleasure exists as a sign of the One in whose arms I will enjoy the only pleasure that can satisfy and give rest to my heart. Pleasure exists to put God in my face and remind me that I was made by him and for him. Pleasure, like every other created thing, was designed to put God at the center, not just of my physical joy but of the deepest thoughts and motives of my heart. Pleasure exists to stimulate worship, not of the thing but of the One who created the thing. The glory of every form of pleasure is meant to point me to the glory of God.

The pleasure of sex is meant to remind me of the glory of my intimate union with Christ, which only grace could produce. The pleasure of food is meant to motivate me to seek the heart-satisfying sustenance of the bread and wine that is Christ. The pleasure of all things beautiful is designed to cause me to gaze upon the Lord, who is perfect in beauty in every way. The pleasure of sound is meant to cause me to listen to the sounds of the One whose every utterance is a thing of beauty. The pleasure of touch was created to remind me of the glory of One whose touch alone has the power to comfort, heal, and transform. The pleasure of human affection is meant to induce me to celebrate the glory of God's eternal, undeserved, self-sacrificing love. The pleasure of rest is meant to draw my heart toward the One who in his life, death, and resurrection purchased for me an eternal sabbath of rest.

Pleasure doesn't detract from God's glory. It doesn't necessarily deaden your heart. Rather, it is one of God's means of reminding you of the satisfying glories that can be found only in him. Pleasure back in Eden and now, like every other created thing, was created to lead you and me to worship.

3. Pleasure demands boundaries.

It is important to recognize that the pleasures of the garden weren't boundless. God set boundaries for Adam and Eve. He gifted them with glorious pleasures to be enjoyed but within the limits he set. They were not to have a self-centered, anytime-anyway relationship to pleasure. They were designed and called to live inside the purpose God had in mind when he made them. Their lives did not belong to them, and neither did their pleasures. They were free to enjoy, but their enjoyment was to be done in an attitude of submission and obedience. The boundaries were a protection. The rules themselves let Adam and Eve know that they weren't in charge. The rules reminded them that they were created for the purposes of another.

The rules weren't pleasure destroying or enjoyment inhibiting. The rules were there to protect the hearts of Adam and Eve so they would be free to liberally enjoy the pleasures of the created world without being dominated, addicted, or controlled by them. The rules were there so they would give themselves not to pleasure but to God, as they enjoyed the beautiful things he had provided. Isn't this a key place where our culture simply gets it wrong? There is an overarching philosophy in Western culture that tells us that authority destroys freedom and rules wreck pleasure. The "pleasure isn't really pleasurable when there are rules attached to it" worldview has been a key ingredient in the insanity that this book is written to address. This view says that eating is no fun if you're being told what to eat. Sex is not enjoyable if you're being told how, when, and with whom you can have it. Creating things of beauty is not satisfying and pleasurable if you have to think about the message communicated by what you create. Eden was the most beautiful place that ever existed, filled with perfect pleasures of every kind, yet its continuance depended on Adam and Eve staying inside God's protective boundaries. It's the horror of the human existence that they decided not to. Boundless pleasure is a deception. By God's design it doesn't exist, and if it did, it could never work.

4. Your life of pleasure is protected only by pleasure.

Your heart and mine are controlled by some kind of pleasure. When your heart is ruled by the desire for a particular kind of pleasure, you can't stop thinking about it, you can't shut off your desire for it, so you will do anything you can to get it. This is a dangerous place to be, and it is a destructive way to live. So if a man's heart is ruled by sexual pleasure, he will put wonderful things in his life at risk in pursuit of this thing he is convinced he cannot live without. Or if someone's heart is ruled by the pleasure of food, he will eat the wrong things way too often and in much too great a quantity. Meanwhile he will ignore the empirical evidence of weight gain, hypertension, and diabetes that are God-given warning signs that he is serving the wrong master.

Only when your heart is mastered by the One who created all the pleasures that so easily addict can your world of pleasure be protected so that you live in balance. Only when your heart is controlled by a higher pleasure, the pleasure of God, can you handle pleasure without being addicted to it. Only when the greatest pleasure in your life is the knowledge that God is pleased by the way you are living can you handle pleasure properly. If the only thing in life that motivates you is your experience of pleasure, you are in pleasure trouble, although you may not yet see the evidence of it. If your principal motive is that God would be pleased, then you can liberally enjoy the variegated pleasures of the created world without rendering yourself fat, addicted, and in debt. When the hearts of Adam and Eve began to be ruled by a pleasurable created thing and not by the One who created it, they quit caring about what pleased God, inserted themselves into the center of the world, wrote their own rules, and created the ultimate human disaster—the fall. We are still among the twisted remains of that horrible choice.

5. When it comes to pleasure, what seems good is often not good.

At some point in the conversation with the Serpent, Eve began to look at a very bad thing and saw it as a very good thing. But the fruit of the forbidden tree with its temporary pleasure was not a good thing to consume. It opened a floodgate of destruction, judgment, and death. Pleasure can be incredibly seductive. Pleasure is often deceptive. Be warned: your pleasures will tell you lies. Your pleasures will make promises they cannot fulfill. Your pleasures will offer you life when in fact they will deliver to you the opposite.

When you are committing an act of gluttony, at that moment you don't see the idolatrous destructiveness of what you're doing. No, you see good—the smells, sights, textures, and flavors of the food. Your problem is that what looks good isn't in fact good.

When you're looking at a sexual website you have no business viewing, you don't see the selfish destructiveness of what you're doing. You are too taken with the erotic beauty of the human form to see that what looks like a good thing is really a very dangerous and destructive thing. When it comes to pleasure, what looks like a good thing may not be a good thing.

So as you're dealing with the basic pleasures that greet you in everyday life, carry the *Eden hermeneutic* with you. Look at pleasure through the interpretive and protective lens of the garden. Understand pleasure, be reminded of its purpose, celebrate its joys, be warned of its danger, and most of all guard your heart.

So Where Do We Go from Here?

Well, there is one final, intensely practical question that needs to be asked. It gets at the heart of how good pleasures become dangerous things. It also gets at the heart of who you are and how you were designed by God to function. Here's the question: What are you asking of your pleasure? You have been designed by God for pleasure. You have been placed by God in a pleasure-saturated world. You have been hardwired with the senses to take in and enjoy the pleasures around you. In short, you are a pleasure seeker. The issue is what kind of pleasures will you give your heart to, and what will you ask of those pleasures?

The good pleasures that God created for our enjoyment and for his glory become bad and dangerous when we ask those pleasures to do for us what they were not intended by God to do. For example, if sex becomes a way by which you establish power, you will do sexual things you should not do, you will use others as objects of your power, and you will leave behind a trail of destruction while you do damage to your own heart. God didn't give you the gift of sexual pleasure so that you could establish personal power and control. I worked in an institution for troubled boys where that was exactly how sex was used. Same-sex rape was a way that older boys established dominance over younger, weaker boys. It was a dark and violent distortion of the pleasurable gift of human sexuality.

If you use wine, which is not in itself an evil thing, as a means of escape from the pressures of life, you are asking wine to do for you what it was not created to do. If wine is your spiritual refuge, you will drink more than you should and, in so doing, compound your problems, while finding neither solutions nor rest for your heart.

There are two observations that flow out of the questions we are considering. The first is that in each instance people are *asking the wrong thing* of pleasure. They are asking it to do the one thing it can never do—satisfy their hearts. The pleasures that God created and embedded in the world he made for us were never intended to be where you and I look for identity, inner rest, contentment, or the stability of well-being that every human seeks. Pleasure will never be your savior. There is a loving, capable, and willing Savior who offers you in his grace everything you need. Pleasure can offer you momentary joy. It can remind you of the greater glory of God, but it must never become your functional God-replacement.

The second observation is that in each instance people are *asking in the wrong way*. The basic approach of people to sex, food, and alcohol puts them in the center of their world. It's a "what I want and what I think I need" approach to life. It doesn't submit to the reality that all pleasure belongs to the Lord. It fails to remember that pleasure had its beginning in the mind of God. It ignores the fact that, like everything else God created, he has a specific purpose for pleasure. So this approach fails to live willingly and joyfully inside God's boundaries.

This way of living descends to the level of "I have a right to be happy and the right to pursue the pleasures that deliver it to me." No matter the confessional theology of the moment, this God-ignoring way of living inserts me in the center of my world, makes my personal definition of happiness paramount, gives me the right to write my own rules, and completely forgets the eternally satisfying pleasures of the love of God that only grace can deliver. And it denies the reality that asking pleasure to do what it was not intended to do never goes anywhere good. When I live for the short-term buzz of any pleasure, because it cannot give me lasting satisfaction I go back again and again, each time wanting more and better, so finding myself controlled by what I once could control. I look around one day, and I'm addicted and enslaved, and pleasure is not what brought me into bondage. No, sadly I did it to myself when I decided to ask something that was designed to remind me of my Savior to be my savior.

While You're Celebrating Pleasure, Celebrate the Cross

It's right to celebrate the goodness of God in giving you sweet pleasures to enjoy, and you should never feel guilty enjoying them as long as you do it within his boundaries and for his glory. It's wonderful to celebrate the tasty pleasures of food, the stunning beauty of a fine piece of art, the sweet intimacy of sex, or the sound drama of a well-written piece of music. But as you're celebrating pleasure, don't forget to celebrate grace.

God's grace has the power to protect you from asking of pleasure what you should not ask. God's grace gives you the power to say no to the seductive call of pleasure when it is vital to say no. God's grace offers you forgiveness when you have failed to do both these things. And God's grace ushers you into the presence of the One who alone can give you the lasting satisfaction and joy that your heart seeks. So as you're celebrating the physical pleasures of the created world, take time to celebrate the eternal pleasures of redemption. And remember to celebrate the fact that as God's child you are heading to a place where pleasure will no longer have any danger attached to it and where your restful heart will not seek what it should not seek.

So when you've had a good meal, your bank account has grown, or you've enjoyed mutual sexual love with your spouse, don't feel guilty. God created pleasure for his glory and your joy. He surrounded you with pleasurable things. He gave you the capacity to enjoy them. You shouldn't feel guilty, but you must remember the tendency of your heart to wander, to replace the Creator with his creation. And remember that a desire for even a good thing becomes a bad thing when it becomes a ruling thing. Be faithful to remind yourself, again and again, that to resist being ruled by what you've been welcomed to enjoy, you've been given forgiving, empowering, transforming, and delivering grace for the battle. Few things argue more strongly for your need of that grace than your struggle to keep God-given pleasures in their proper place.

Review and Reflect

1. How would you summarize the *Eden hermeneutic*? How can understanding its meaning aid you in day-to-day life?

2. What is asceticism, and why is it ineffective in keeping us from sexual sin? How do the following passages serve as a corrective?

   • Ecclesiastes 2:24

   • 1 Timothy 6:17

   • Hebrews 11:25–26

   • James 1:17

3. How is pleasure linked to the glory of God, and how can we participate in showcasing this link?

4. How do boundaries enhance rather than diminish pleasure?

5. In what area or areas of life are you prone to addiction, and how can you avoid such enslavement?

Heart Reset

   • Genesis 2:15–3:24

6

Sex: The Big Picture

Jim was thirteen years old, and something had been awakened in him. He was not sure what it was, but he liked it. He liked it a lot. It happened to him when he looked at pictures of women in magazines. It happened to him as he walked by those lingerie stores at the mall. It happened when he quietly surfed his way onto certain websites. He felt the buzz, and he liked it. And all he knew was that it felt good, and he wanted more.

- - -

Aaron didn't really care about how comfortable his wife was. He didn't really think much about what was good and enjoyable for her. He didn't really think about the gentle, tender, relational aspect of intimacy. Aaron thought this way: "I'm married, and sex is my right, no holds barred." He felt that Ginger should be ready any time he requested sex and that she should do whatever it was that brought him pleasure. If he came home in the middle of the day and was ready, then it was her responsibility to be willing.

But Ginger felt like an object, a plaything for Aaron's pleasure. She felt put upon and demanded of. Sex was for her increasingly less often an act of mutual love. It had become a daily obligation, one she frequently dreaded. And to make matters worse, she was uncomfortable with the things Aaron was asking her to do, not to mention afraid that he seemed increasingly obsessed with sex. She had tried to get Aaron to talk with her about their sexual life, but he told her he thought everything was cool. She had tried to share her feelings with him, but he didn't seem to listen. She had tried refusing his advances at points, but he only got angry and accused her of being selfish. Aaron was demanding what Ginger dreaded, and she just didn't know what to do.

– – –

Mandy was in college, and she loved every minute of the experience. For the first time in her life she felt independent and attractive. She loved the attention she was getting from the guys in her dorm and in her classes. Her first two years had been a whirlwind of classes, dating, and short-term romances. She was maintaining her grades and occasionally thought about her future, but that's not what kept her going; the social scene was. Her weekends began on Thursday night and didn't end until very late on Sunday. On Monday the plan for the next weekend was already forming.

Mandy loved the fact that she didn't feel awkward anymore. She liked the way her body had developed, and she liked the fact that her looks got her lots of male attention. She felt alive and appreciated. Although she was uncomfortable with some of the things her romantic partners wanted her to do, she loved that she was so attractive that guys were always after her.

In ways that Mandy was not conscious of, she dressed not so much to cover or adorn her body as to expose and draw attention to it. Mandy was not scared about being thought of as a slut. What really scared her was being thought of as a prude by any of the guys. With makeup too heavy and clothes too tight she would begin each day expecting and reveling in the attention she got as she made her way around the campus. Her way of responding to the guys around her was flirtatious and seductive, but she would deny it when confronted. She saw herself as a normal twenty-year-old girlie girl getting in touch with her emotions and her body. If asked about her lifestyle she would say, "Lots of fun, little harm."

- - -

Gerrard had made the decision, and for him there was no turning back. He told himself that he was simply being true to his feeling, true to the way he had been put together. He knew his parents would be upset, but he was tired of living in the shadows and covering his tracks. He wasn't going to do it anymore. He knew what turned him on and what didn't. He knew whom he was attracted to and whom he wasn't. He knew the kind of life he wanted and the kind he wanted to avoid. With his decision made, he felt quite liberated.

Gerrard was attracted to men. He told himself that he had always been that way. He had come to see denying it as stupid and immature. He thought the people around him had no right to question it. And he was convinced it was a colossal waste of time to fight it. This weekend, while with his parents, he was going to declare his sexual orientation and his love for David. He didn't want to needlessly hurt his parents, but they would just have to come to terms with who he was and how he had decided to live his life. He thought of himself as a Christian, but he had little time for what the Bible had to say about his lifestyle choice. He wasn't going to bow to the "ancient chauvinism of biblical times." He said he loved God, and he was content with the kind of person God had made him to be. He didn't feel the need to change anything.

- - -

Teddy hated old age, and he hated being alone. He hated not having a companion to share his life with, but if he were willing to be honest, what he really hated was the loss of his sexual life. He couldn't stop thinking about it. It made no sense to him, and it made him bitter. He was fully alive and virile but had no sex in his future. It made no sense that God would design him with this kind of body and these kinds of desires but forbid him to express them simply because his wife had died and he was alone. What was he supposed to do with his feelings and urges? "Yes, I'm old, but I'm not dead," he would say to himself.

He envied the young couples at church and fantasized about their sex life. He looked at the younger women and wondered if any would ever be attracted to him. He felt that his life at this point was a sick joke or maybe a divine punishment of some kind. He couldn't imagine continuing to live like this. He'd rather be dead.

- - -

Heather had no sexual attraction to her husband whatsoever. Since they had gotten married he had put on about thirty-five pounds. The athletic body of the man she'd married had given way to this pudgy guy who spent most of his time at home sitting in warmups, watching the sports he no longer had the energy to play. When Heather saw his body, she was turned off. When they attempted to have sex, all she could think of was the size of his belly. She would occasionally succumb to his advances, but it was all she could do to fake her way through and make sure he was satisfied enough to leave her alone for a few days.

Heather fantasized about being married to a fit and handsome man. She dreamed about having sex and feeling muscles rather than flab. She was unhappy, and she felt trapped. It all made her angry. She couldn't imagine living the rest of her life this way. She had sexual desires that needed to be satisfied, but not by Lumpy (the rather cruel nickname Heather had given her husband). In fact, when she had sex with her husband, Heather would often get through it by fantasizing that she was with someone else. She found herself absorbing more of the romance novels that seemed to be everywhere. She built a vicarious sexual life, living in worlds of attraction and seduction that didn't exist but that took her away from the prison she had gotten herself into.

There was no self-conscious, point-in-time decision, but Heather began to plan her escape. She thought about what she would say to her husband and how she would break the news to her family. She wondered how she would support herself and where she would live. She worried about whether there would be a big battle for the kids. She wanted to feel attractive again, and she wanted to be attracted to someone. She wanted sex where she could really give herself rather than just pretend. She was tired of doing things that revolted her with someone who repulsed her. And Heather just couldn't imagine that this was how God wanted her to live. She didn't know how, and she hadn't yet considered when, but she knew that somehow, someway she was getting out.

Little-Picture Sex

All the people about whom I have just written are suffering from the same thing. It is more powerful than they know; it has made sex to be something that it isn't and has created deep dissatisfaction in all of them. What shapes, controls, and ultimately distorts their sexuality, making a beautiful thing a dark and painful thing, is *little-picture sex*.

Sex is not a thing unto itself that can exist by itself. Sex, by design, is meant to be connected. It is meant to be tied to and understood in relation to big things of huge and consequential proportion. *Big-picture sex* is understood as being part of how life was designed and what it is meant to be. *Little-picture sex*, because it is isolated, gets kidnapped by desires and agendas that rob it of its original purpose. *Big-picture sex* acknowledges that there is something bigger than personal physical pleasure. *Little-picture sex* exists in the small confines of what will give me pleasure at this point in my life. *Big-picture sex* serves something bigger. *Little-picture sex* is owned by the individual and is entitled and demanding. *Big-picture sex* willingly submits to rules. *Little-picture sex* writes its own rules. *Big-picture sex* is driven by a commitment to others. *Little-picture sex* is dominated by the pleasures of self. *Big-picture sex* is patient and kind. *Little-picture sex* makes impatient demands and punishes people when they don't come through. *Big-picture sex* is viewed as a part of life. *Little-picture sex* tends to take over your life. *Big-picture sex* contributes to deeper love and worship. *Little-picture sex* leads to relational hurt and vertical rebellion. God designed sex to be inextricably connected to things of consequence. It doesn't work any other way.

Our Sex Problems Aren't First Physical

My wife, Luella, and I love art museums. We love post-war abstraction. We love what shape, color, texture, and light can communicate when juxtaposed in an interesting, provocative, or beautiful way.

I had seen a detail of a work we wanted to see, and I hadn't been impressed. (A detail is a section of a painting used for announcement and advertising purposes.) The artist was one of the greats, so I was willing to go check out the exhibit anyway. When I saw the painting from which they had taken the detail, I was blown away. I couldn't stop looking at it. The detail had melted into the painting—it wasn't the thing that stood out—but the painting would not have looked the same without it.

So it is with sex. When it exists as an isolated, disconnected part of our lives, it not only loses its contextual beauty but begins to be known and understood as something it's not. Here's why human sexuality must be understood and experienced from the vantage point of the *big picture*. You and I simply need to humbly admit that the things that make sex gorgeous, exciting, and fulfilling as per God's design are not natural and intuitive to us. It's intuitive to be self-oriented, entitled, and demanding. It's natural to want to write our own rules. It's normal to act as if our bodies belong to us. It's intuitive to think that the goal of life is to experience our personal definition of happiness and pleasure. It's natural to see others as a means of our own happiness. It's normal to think of life in physical and material terms. It's intuitive to live for the moment. It's intuitive to practically forget God's existence and to live a life dominated by horizontal concerns. It's natural to try to work the people around us into a willingness to deliver to us what would make us happy. It's comfortable to think more in terms of "I want" than "I should." I remind you that what distorts sex, what has the power to make it hurtful and dark, is not first the physical demands we make on one another or the way we physically use one another. What puts sex on a pathway that it was never meant to travel is something deeply spiritual. Our biggest sex problems lurk inside us; they're not the result of a culture that has gone sexually insane. The culture has become sexually insane because of what lurks inside us.

Now, I know that this will be a struggle for some of you to get on board with. I know it will make some of you angry, and some of you will read with hurt feelings, but what I'm about to say needs to be said. What I just described are the normal characteristics of *little-picture sex*. They are also the very things that twist and distort the beautiful creation of God and press it into something it was never intended to be. Yes, *little-picture sex* is still sex, but it is carnival-mirror, distorted sex. So here's the humbling admission: apart from God's grace rescuing us from us, the things that are natural and intuitive are the very things that rust and ruin sex. None of us comes to sex with a neutral heart. None of us approaches sex free of the me-ism of the sinful nature. None of us comes to sex morally pure. None of us is free from the temptation to insert ourselves in the middle of our world, making it all about us. None of us. You can't just run with what is natural, because what is natural to you as a sinner will invariably start you in a different direction from what the Creator designed as good.

Sex exposes our hearts, and in exposing our hearts, it reminds us of our deep and comprehensive need for God's forgiving, transforming, and ultimately delivering grace. In his grace God has entered our struggle with sex and done two things for us. First, he has given us the big picture. It's that thirty-thousand-foot view of life that is the grand sweep of Scripture. In this way the Bible doesn't simply define the religious domain of our life; it redefines and reorients every single thing in our life, including our sexuality. But God has done more than just that, as important as his Word is. He gave us Jesus, who entered our struggle, lived as we couldn't live, died the death we should have died, and rose, defeating death, so that we would have everything we need to live as God intended—yes, live as God intended, even in our sexual lives.

So What Does Big-Picture Sex Look Like?

As I stated before, *big-picture sex* is connected sex. And what is it connected to? It is connected to the things that God lovingly reveals in his Word as being vital and important. If you don't look at sex (or anything else in your life) through the lens of these things, then whatever you're looking at, you haven't seen correctly. If your way of thinking about your own sexuality, or if your sexual desires or your definition of good sex, doesn't include these things, then your thinking will be inherently wrong at some point or at some level. Let's consider these things.

1. Sex is connected to God's existence.

Since God created both you and sex, it is impossible to properly understand sex and participate in it appropriately if you are practically ignoring God and his existence. By means of creation you are his, and your sex life is his. This means that you do not have a natural right to do with your life and your body as you please. You are not entitled to an autonomous pursuit of happiness. In fact, you don't have autonomy. Your life came from him and belongs to him. Sex connects you to God, whether or not you recognize it. The way you express your sexuality will either recognize God's existence and honor him or deny his existence and rebel against his authority. If the latter, then sex will reveal that you think you have liberty you do not have, rights you have never been given, and authority that only ever belongs to the Creator.

Sex that recognizes God's existence becomes the beautiful,

intimate, relational act of worship that it was intended to be. In the midst of all its physical delights, it does not forget God. It remembers that everything enlivened and enjoyed in sex belongs to him. It rests in his control and celebrates his care in the midst of the most intimate of human connections. I will say much more about this in chapters to come.

2. Sex is connected to God's glory.

Creation isn't ultimate. The joys of creation were designed by God to be enjoyable, but that joy wasn't designed to be ultimate. All the joys of creation are meant to direct you toward greater joy. All the glories of the created world are meant to produce in you a hunger for greater glory and to point you to where that glory can be found. All the intimate physical and emotional glories of sex are meant to point you to the one glory for which you were created to live and through which your heart will be fulfilled.

Now, this immediately tells you two very practical things. First, sex cannot and will not ever satisfy your heart. The purpose of sex is not to bring you to a point of spiritual satisfaction. Maybe you're thinking, "Paul, what in the world are you talking about? Nobody hopes sex will do that." In fact, I am convinced that many, many people do. They look for sex to do something that it was never designed to do. I counseled a woman who said she had had sex with at least a hundred men, and she told me that she would do anything (sexual) to hear a man whisper in her ear, "I love you." Do you see what she was doing? She was hoping to get identity, value, and that inner sense of peace through sex. Sex couldn't do for her what she wanted it to do, so she had to go back again and again, each time getting further from her goal. Sex would never deliver what she was asking; only the God who created sex could, and sex was created to point to him.

But something foundational must be understood here. In our sexual life we must be propelled by a greater glory than our own. Sex *is* glorious, and it makes us feel powerful, connected, and alive. But we must not own these glories for ourselves alone. We were created to live in the most intimate and personal places of our lives for a glory bigger than our own, the glory of God. You may be thinking, "Like, how in the world do you do that in the middle of foreplay or intercourse?" Keep reading; the chapters that follow will unpack this even more practically.

3. Sex is connected to God's purpose.

You and I do not live by instinct. We are purpose-oriented beings by God's design. Everything you do, you do for a reason, whether or not you are aware of that. In sex you are always motivated by purpose. Perhaps your only purpose is personal erotic pleasure. Perhaps your purpose is mutual erotic satisfaction. Perhaps your purpose is more frequent sexual intercourse. None of these things is evil in itself if it is connected to and protected by the larger purpose of God. As we said earlier, everything made by God's hands was made for a purpose. So in sex, as in everything else, you must ask, "What is God's purpose for this compelling, intimate human relationship?"

One reason that sex gets distorted and becomes something God never intended and ends up being hurtful, dark, and dangerous is that in this fallen world, it is most often motivated by no larger purpose than the pleasure of the individual. So selfish teenage boys coerce their girlfriends into oral sex. Materialistic women see pornography as a way of making a lot of money quickly. Married men use their wife for their pleasure with little regard for her feeling loved and cared for. Single women use their sexuality to get attention and acceptance. Unmarried people surf the Internet for sexual pleasure. Middle school boys spend secret time in the locker room making rude and immature sex jokes. Advertisers use sex to sell just about anything. Powerful men use their power to get what belongs to someone else.

Sex is only ever safe when everything we think, desire, say, and do in our sexual lives is directed and protected by the clear purpose of God as revealed in his Word, which leads us to our next point.

4. Sex is connected to God's revelation.

The God who created this world and acts to hold it together not only acts, but he speaks. He has spoken in his Word. This revelation of him, his plan, and his purpose for the world is meant to be the ultimate, overarching interpreter of life. In God's Word I come to know who he is, who I am, and what in the world life is about. In God's Word I learn about what sex is and who it is for. In God's Word I learn the attitudes, choices, and actions that cause sex to be the holy thing God created it to be. And in God's Word I learn how sin distorts sex, what God forbids, and the temptations that must be avoided in submission to God and for the protection of self.

You could argue that the Bible is a manual on sex. To the degree that it lays out God's original purpose for sex, details how sin redirects the thoughts and motives of my heart, details what God has commanded and forbidden, offers me case studies, and points to the necessary rescue of grace—to that degree it gives me all the essential heart and life information I need to be what I am supposed to be and do what I am supposed to do in this critical area of human life.

Sex is dangerous when it is pursued outside of the critical information that you can get only through divine revelation. You cannot get it by means of individual experience or collective research. After all, God made you; he is not surprised that you are a sexual being. So as in other critical areas of your life, he has spoken to you about sex with words of wisdom and grace that you will hear nowhere else.

5. Sex is connected to God's redemption.

Sex takes place between the already and the not yet. Already Jesus has come, already the Word has been given, already the Spirit has been sent, but not yet has the world been restored, not yet has sin been eradicated, and not yet have you and I been finally delivered from sin. So our lives as sexual beings are lived out in the middle of a dramatically broken world that cries out for redemption. Until this world is fully restored by its Savior Creator to the condition for which it was created, seductive temptations, deceit, destruction, and death will live. Your world of sexuality will be one of temptation, where deceitful voices make promises that they cannot deliver, wooing you outside the boundaries of God's wise purpose and plan.

In this world of temptation you will see things that you were not meant to lay your eyes on. You will be told things that simply are not true. You will be offered things that you must not accept. You will be exposed to sex being used in ways God never intended. What is dangerous will be presented to you as healthy and right, and what is wrong in the eyes of God will be held before you as right and good. What you learn about sex will be full of inaccuracies and distortions. You will barely be able to live a single day without having your morals assaulted or challenged in some way.

But there is another fundamental reality between the already and the not yet. It is that sin still lives with power inside you. Your problem is not just that you live in a broken world where temptation lurks all around you; your problem is that you are susceptible to that temptation because of the moral iniquity that still exists in your heart. I have said this before, but it bears repeating here: it is only ever the evil inside us that hooks us to the evil outside us. That is what the Bible means when it says that to the pure all things are pure (Titus 1:15).

But I am not pure. By God's grace I am growing in purity, but I'm not there yet, so I carry around in me a vulnerability to temptation. I am capable of longing for things that I should immediately resist. I am susceptible to desiring things that I should actually hate. I am tempted to look intently at what I should close my eyes to. And with all of this, I am able to swindle myself into thinking that I am okay, that what I have desired or done is not that bad after all.

Sex really does expose the deep and sinful selfishness of our hearts. It really does show us that at the intersection of hunger and temptation we are quite capable of being disloyal and rebellious. It does reveal that our pleasures are often more valuable to us than God's purposes. Sex does expose that desires for autonomy and self-sovereignty are still inside of us. Sex does demonstrate that I don't always love my neighbor as myself, that, in fact, I am still willing at points to use another human being for my own purposes and pleasures. Sex shows how easy it is to function as a God-amnesiac, even though in my theology I recognize his existence.

All this means that sex immediately connects me to my own and the world's need for redemption. The hope for sex in human culture is not more prevalent sex education and better contraception. The hope for sex in human culture is not a thing; it is a person, and his name is Jesus. Sex groans for redemption and, in groaning for redemption, reaches out for the Savior. And human sexuality will only ever fully be what it was intended to be when he has finally made all things new.

6. Sex is connected to God's eternity.

Finally, sex connects you to eternity and your need for the kingdom to come. Sex cannot be divorced from God's eternal plan. You and I must not live in this moment in time as if it is all there is. There is more and better to come. So what is this moment of sex about? This moment of sex is not a destination but part of preparing you for the final destination. All the struggles of sexuality are not in the way of God's plan but part of it. God knew he was leaving us in this fallen world for a period of time. He knew well what we would face here. All the messiness between the already and the not yet is meant, in the hands of God, to be transformational, that we would through difficulty and trial become people ready for the eternity all his redeemed children will spend with him.

But there is more. God has hardwired eternity into all of our hearts. That means there is a desire for paradise in all of us. But you will not experience paradise in the here and now. And if you try to turn this present moment into the paradise you long for, you will be anxious, controlling, disappointed, frustrated, demanding, and ultimately discouraged and bitter. Your husband or wife will never be the perfect lover. You will never experience paradise sex in the here and now. Celebrate the good things God gives you in the here and now, be content, and keep reminding yourself that you are being prepared for the wonderful eternity to come.

- - -

The problem is that nobody connected sex for Hank. His sexual awakening took place one afternoon when he happened upon a secret stash of '70s-era girlie magazines that his father had hidden for years. He was immediately alive and magnetized. He didn't understand what had just happened to him, but he wanted more. It was a sad, seductive welcome to the world of *little-picture sex*. It was pleasure for pleasure's sake, sex for sex's sake. Over the next two years, Hank visited that hidden stash almost daily. Before long he was trying to sneak kisses from the girls at school or cop a feel where it seemed possible. He stole porn from the local newsstand and sought out art movies with nudity.

His college years consisted of sexual fantasy and conquest. He probably thought about sex more than about his studies, but he didn't see himself as in trouble. In his senior year, through a campus ministry, he made a profession of faith. He quickly learned that he could not do the things he had been doing. But his obsession did not go away, and he failed again and again. And despite all the do's and don'ts he submitted to, his view of sex was still pretty much isolated, *little-picture sex.* It makes sense that the desire for marriage would grow in Hank. It was the one way that sex was "legal," although he did not know the extent to which that really motivated him. He also thought that getting married would solve his sex problems by giving him regular satisfaction.

But marriage didn't solve Hank's problem. It wasn't long before his wife felt that she was being used rather than loved, and it didn't take long for Hank to begin to live a secret life of illicit sex. When Suzy found his Internet stash, she was devastated but not surprised.

Hank then faced the depth of his need—no, not just for a more biblically sexual worldview, but his need for grace. When viewed properly, sex always connects you to the existence and plan of God; it connects you to the fact that you and everything in your life were made for him and that you cannot be what you are supposed to be or do what you are supposed to do without his grace. Now, it may seem weird to some of you and irreverent to others, but it needs to be said: when viewed properly, sex preaches the gospel of Jesus Christ. Sex tells you how broken the world is, and it tells you how weak and rebellious you are. In telling you these things, it points you to your need for a Savior and to the hope that is found not in better education or firmer human resolve but in his forgiving, transforming, empowering, and delivering grace.

Big-picture sex acknowledges God, admits to sin, and celebrates grace and so grows in both purity and contentment. *Little-picture sex* lives in disconnected denial and never goes anywhere good. Where does your sexuality live?

Review and Reflect

1. List the criteria of both little-picture sex and big-picture sex. Which criteria strike you most forcefully and why?

2. Sex is integrally connected to God in vital ways. Write a summary statement for each of these ways:

   God's existence:

   God's glory:

   God's purpose:

   God's revelation:

   God's redemption:

   God's eternity:

3. How would you define your purpose in life, and how has this definition shaped your sexuality? Identify ways in which your personal pursuits fail to align with God's purpose for you. How does 1 Corinthians 6:18–20 guide you in getting realigned?

4. What did the apostle Paul mean when he wrote, "To the pure, all things are pure" (Titus 1:15)?

5. How has a longing for paradise impacted your sex life both in the past and in the present?

Heart Reset

- 1 Corinthians 7:1–5

- Titus 1:15

7

If Sex Is about Worship, Then It Can't Be Just about You

So where has all this sexual insanity come from? What is the root cause? Again, this insanity is not the fault of the entertainment, advertising, fashion, or Internet industries. The cause is much more foundational. Whether it's the executive who uses sex to sell a product and increase his bottom line and personal success, the teenager using sex for another immature thrill, the old man grabbing at his nurse, the young woman who uses sex to get at the riches of an old man, the husband having sex with someone other than his wife, or the ratings-obsessed TV executive throwing sex into a sitcom even though it is not necessary to the plotline, each person is doing the same thing. In ways that they do not understand, they are part of the insanity. In fact, each is doing something that drives the sexual insanity we find everywhere around us.

All of them are taking sex as their own, acting as if it belongs to them and using it for whatever purpose they choose. Sex becomes their possession, their product, and their tool. It's a "sex is all about me" view of human sexuality. I am deeply persuaded that the insanity of sex that marks human culture is the direct result of the *individualization* of sex. It's sex for my purpose, my pleasure, according to my plan. This is what the next three chapters will address. Sex according to God's wise and gracious design simply cannot be just about me. This *individualization* of sex cannot work. It will never result in sex being what God intended. It will never keep sex from distortion and darkness. It will never protect sex from misuse and abuse. *Individualized* sex simply cannot and will not go anywhere good.

The *individualization* of sex violates three fundamental biblical principles: worship, relationship, and obedience. The next three chapters will look at sex from the vantage point of these three principles.

Sex Is an Act of Worship

They are two words that may seem strange when placed side by side: *sex* and *worship*. It's intuitive to understand these two words as capturing two separate and very different worlds. But worship and sex properly understood cannot be separated. Sex is an act of worship, and the true worship of God will determine what happens in your sexual life. In fact, even the most irreligious person expresses worship every time he engages in some kind of sexual activity, whether mental or physical. Let me say it this way: in sex you are always worshiping something. Your sexual life is shaped by the worship of God, the worship of self, the worship of your sexual partner, or the worship of what you get out of sex. This means that in sex you and I surrender our hearts to something. The things we say, do, and seek in sex are all ruled by the desire for something. In this most intimate of human activities, you reveal who God designed you to be—a worshiper. You don't put down your worship nature when you're having sex. You and I have worshiped our way through every moment of any kind of sexual activity to which we've given ourselves.

Think for a moment about how your sexual life would change if you took the worship nature of your humanity seriously. Think of what a difference it would make if you always connected sex to worship. Think of what would change in your sexual thoughts, desires, choices, and actions. You see, if sex is all about you worshiping you ("I want to rule my life and do what I want to do"), it will never work as God intended. If sex is all about you worshiping your partner ("I can't live without the love of this other person"), sex will never work as God intended. Or if sex is all about worshiping what you get out of sex ("I can't live without what sex does for me"), it will never work as God intended. Worship of anything other than God always ends in the worship of self and the *individualization* of things that are designed by God to connect us to things that are bigger than our wants, needs, and pleasures.

There is a passage in the New Testament that gets to the practical core of what it means to connect sex and worship. It lays out what it means to approach your sexuality as a worshiper of God and to practically acknowledge that if sex is all about worship, it can't be just about you. Read carefully the words of this passage:

> "All things are lawful for me," but not all things are helpful. "All things are lawful for me," but I will not be dominated by anything. "Food is meant for the stomach and the stomach for food"—and God will destroy both one and the other. The body is not meant for sexual immorality, but for the Lord, and the Lord for the body. And God raised the Lord and will also raise us up by his power. Do you not know that your bodies are members of Christ? Shall I then take the members of Christ and make them members of a prostitute? Never! Or do you not know that he who

is joined to a prostitute becomes one body with her? For, as it is written, "The two will become one flesh." But he who is joined to the Lord becomes one spirit with him. Flee from sexual immorality. Every other sin a person commits is outside the body, but the sexually immoral person sins against his own body. Or do you not know that your body is a temple of the Holy Spirit within you, whom you have from God? You are not your own, for you were bought with a price. So glorify God in your body. (1 Cor. 6:12–20)

Paul looks at the subject of sex through the lens of four worship principles and two worship commands. Each one of the worship principles points you to your identity as a child of God:

- Mastery: I have been designed for worship.
- Eternity: I have been hardwired for eternity.
- Unity: Grace has made me one with Jesus Christ.
- Ownership: I am now the property of Christ.

The apostle's words in 1 Corinthians 6 are as helpful and as practical a discussion of the implications of worship on the most intimate and personal areas of life as you will find in all of Scripture. I think that for years I had an unbiblical view of my own sexuality. I'm not talking about sexual sin in my life. I'm talking about a failure to have a robustly biblical view of this very important part of human existence. My biblical view of sex was limited to a catalog of things that God said I could not do. It was a boundary view of the Bible and sex. It was as if all the Bible did was define the boundaries you must stay inside. So I thought that as long as I stayed inside of God's boundaries, sex belonged to me for my pleasure. I think many, many Christians hold this view. They wrongly think that the Bible's relation to sex is regulatory and little else. But this legal understanding of the Bible and sex didn't help or protect me as I thought it would.

The law of God is excellent when it comes to exposing sin. God's law is a wonderful guide for how you were designed to live your life. But the law has no power to defeat sin or deliver you from it. The problem with viewing the Bible as a book of sex boundaries is that you don't then seek or get biblical help for where the sexual struggle actually takes place. My problem isn't that I am ignorant of what God says is right or wrong when it comes to sex; my problem is that even in the face of knowing what is right and wrong, I still desire and do things I shouldn't. My problem is that there are times when I don't care what God says is right or wrong. I want what I want. I will have what I will have. I will use what has been given for whatever purpose I choose. It is this deeper struggle that I need help with. It is because of this deeper struggle that Jesus had to come. You could argue that Jesus came to rescue sex or, maybe more explicitly, in sex to rescue you from you. Paul's discussion roots at this deeper level.

Sex and Four Inescapable Worship Principles
1. The Principle of Mastery
The principle of mastery is the principle of principles. It addresses design, struggle, and solution. You simply cannot understand the sexual struggle and how it is solved without understanding this principle. Hear Paul's words again: "'All things are lawful for me,' but not all things are helpful. 'All things are lawful for me,' but I will not be dominated by anything. 'Food is meant for the stomach and the stomach for food'—and God will destroy both one and the other. The body is not meant for sexual immorality, but for the Lord, and the Lord for the body" (1 Cor. 6:12–13). Let's unpack the thunderous importance of these little sentences.

When Paul says, "All things are lawful for me," he is not giving his worldview; he is parroting the misconception of people around him. Classic antinomianism would say that because Christ fulfilled the law, I do not have to live its requirements anymore. I am free from the law, bottom line. Yes, I am free from the requirements of the law in terms of earning acceptance with God, but I am not free from the law in terms of its being God's ordained moral claim on my life as his creature. But Paul's answer to this false-gospel worldview is even more forceful and eloquent than a mere critique of this misunderstanding of the work of Christ and God's law. He essentially responds this way: "Even if everything were legal, I would still have a big problem, because when it comes to sex I don't have just a legal problem; I have a mastery problem. Because of my mastery problem, even God's good things become bad things because they become ruling things. My struggle is deeper than an ignorance or misunderstanding of God's law. My problem is that there are moments when I am a rebel against God's law because I have given over my heart to another master."

Paul is saying, "When it comes to things like sex, my problem is a fickle, wandering, easily disloyal heart. I say that Jesus is my Lord, but I am daily tempted to give my heart over to the rule of other masters." You see, between the already and the not yet, every day is a mastery struggle. Every day in every area of my life a battle of rulers wages in my heart. Every day I am tempted to shift masters. Every day I am tempted to tell myself that it is okay to give my heart to a master other than Jesus for just a few minutes; after all, in the grand scheme of things what difference will it make?

Sex is one in a list of a whole catalog of good things that can become bad things when they become ruling things. If you allow your heart to be ruled by sex or sexual pleasure or sexual power or whatever other thing sex gets you, you will not only misuse this good gift of God but also end up being controlled by it. Sexual distortion and addiction exist not because sex itself is bad but because we have put it in a place that God never intended.

So what do we do about this mastery struggle? What do we do

about our fickle, wandering hearts? How do we protect ourselves from the insanity of being mastered by something other than the one true Master? Well, let's go back to Paul's words again.

Why does he insert, "'Food is meant for the stomach and the stomach for food'—and God will destroy both one and the other"? Here Paul recites a second popular misconception that essentially says, "It doesn't make any difference what you do with your body because your body and what fills it will all be destroyed anyway."

And as he did with the first misconception, Paul answers this false-gospel worldview with the principle of mastery. What you do with your body right here and right now does matter, because your body has a master—the Lord himself. You can never properly understand the gospel of Jesus Christ and conclude that what you do with your body is your business or what you do with your body doesn't matter. Jesus gives you his grace not to free you to live as though you're king but to live in the freedom of honoring him as your King.

Now what does all this have to do with sex? The answer is, everything. Sex is one area where I most powerfully and practically reveal what truly rules my heart. My sex life is shaped and directed by whatever is my street-level master. And I will only ever stay inside of God's wise boundaries when he is the functional ruler of my heart. Does that discourage you? It does me! Because I don't do very well at keeping God central in my life all the time every day. I am very skilled at convincing myself that there are things I deserve or things I cannot live without. I am very skilled at convincing myself that this little trespass, just this once, isn't such a big deal. I don't know how to keep my heart from being fickle. I don't think I have the power to keep myself safe.

Here is where this first principle preaches the gospel to us. My hope in the struggle for sexual purity or any other victory over sin is found not in my perfect submission to Christ as my master but in his perfect submission to the will of the Father on my behalf. In my sin, weakness, and struggle I do not have to be paralyzed by fear or hide in shame. I can stand before a holy God, broken as I am, and cry out for his forgiveness, help, protection, and rescue. And I do not have to fear his rejection, because my standing before him is based on the righteousness of the Savior, not on my own righteousness.

But there is something else. The gospel of Jesus Christ also guarantees me help in this struggle of mastery. Jesus is with me, in me, and for me. He fights on my behalf even when I fail to have the sense or the willingness to fight. Now that's hope!

2. The Principle of Eternity

This second worship principle, the principle of eternity, is of equal significance. Hear the words of Paul again: "And God raised the Lord and will also raise us up by his power" (1 Cor. 6:14). Why does Paul interject this little sentence about the resurrection of Jesus and our future resurrection? The answer is that Paul knows himself, and he knows his audience. A core issue in the sexual struggle is our tendency to treat a particular moment of life as if it is all there is, all that we have. Permit me to recap.

By God's design you and I are hardwired for eternity. That means that every human being carries around a desire for paradise. So there are only two ways to live. Either you think that this is all there is and therefore take control of your life and relationships and try to turn this moment into the eternity it will never be, or you understand that this moment isn't your final destination but a preparation for a destination to come.

These are two vastly different ways of living. The first person tells himself that he's only going to go around once, so he'd better get all the pleasure he possibly can before death takes him out of the game; and the other person recognizes the brokenness of the world, the temporary and unfulfilling pleasures of the here and now, and looks forward to the eternal joys of the forever that is to come. Eternity amnesia makes a mess out of sex. It puts the focus on present pleasure rather than on eternal joy. It causes us to be driven rather than patient and restful. It diminishes the eternal significance of little decisions, making life more about what we've been able to experience than about how we have lived. It causes us to replace the focus on God's purpose for creating us with a focus on our personal pleasure. It makes us hope for a satisfaction we won't find this side of eternity and to look for it in places it simply cannot be found.

It may sound weird to you, but you and I were meant to have sex (inside of God's boundaries) with eternity in view. We were meant to know that sex will never be the paradise we are searching for. We were meant to understand that sex will never satisfy our hearts. We were meant to understand that a particular moment is more about the hardship of preparation than about the quest for personal pleasure. Our sexual lives were meant to be protected by the long view of life. Living with eternity in view is one thing God uses to direct and purify our sexual existence. Between the already and the not yet, it is far better for our sexual life to be lived on the basis of restful hope (the best is yet to come) than on fearful hunger (this is all we have; we'd better get all we can).

If you're God's child, the resurrection of Jesus guarantees you a future way beyond the glory of any pleasures you will experience in this right-here, right-now broken world. Again, Jesus lived with eternity in view in every way, and he did this on your behalf and for your benefit so that you would have the grace you need to live for something bigger than the temporary pleasures of the here and now, including sex.

3. The Principle of Unity

Here, in the principle of unity, Paul puts forth one of the most precious mysteries of the gospel. Hear his words:

> Do you not know that your bodies are members of Christ? Shall I then take the members of Christ and make them members of a prostitute? Never! Or do you not know that he who is joined to a prostitute becomes one body with her? For, as it is written, "The two will become one flesh." But he who is joined to the Lord becomes one spirit with him. Flee from sexual immorality. Every other sin a person commits is outside the body, but the sexually immoral person sins against his own body. (1 Cor. 6:15–18)

With language that is shocking and sobering, Paul reminds us of something we must always remember as we deal with the relationships, pleasures, and temptations of this here-and-now fallen world. If you are God's child, you have been united to Christ. This is not just an amorphous spiritual reality but a physical one as well. All of what makes you *you* has been united to Christ. Your emotionality, your physicality, your mentality, your personality, your psychology, and your spirituality have all been united to Christ.

This means that you take Christ with you wherever you are and into whatever you are doing. Union with Christ means your life isn't bifurcated. You don't have Christ and the spiritual part of your life alongside of everything else. He *is your life*. It's Christ in and with you in the most intimate, secret, and, yes, even dark moments of your life. He is united to every thought and desire. He is connected to every fantasy and choice. He is there during every action and reaction.

So Paul asks the key question, "Shall I then take the members of Christ [the parts of my body] and make them members of a prostitute?" (v. 15). What a perspective on sexual sin! It is much, much more than a breaking of some ancient abstract law that God decided to lay on us. No, for me as a believer, sexual sin is a horrific violation of my relationship with Christ. It is to love my pleasure so deeply that I am willing to connect the Holy One to what is unholy. Paul is describing an unthinkable act of selfishness, disloyalty, and rebellion. Since I am one with Christ, and since sex creates a one-flesh bond with a prostitute, I am essentially in my selfishness willing to unite Christ to a prostitute. No wonder Paul says, "Never!" (v. 15).

I am deeply persuaded that there are few things more protective and purifying to keep in mind as you deal with sexual desire and temptation than the reality and totality of your union with your Savior. Jesus Christ is in you and you in him, even in the most secret and holy moments of your sexual life. And he is with you as well in the most unholy moments.

Does this make you afraid? Ashamed? Guilty? Paralyzed? This beautiful union with Christ, which only grace could create, also guarantees you all the grace you need to live within that reality. It guarantees all the grace you need to wage war with your desires. It gives all the grace you need to say no to what is unholy and yes to what is pleasing in the eyes of him to whom you are united. And it offers you the forgiveness you will need as you fail once again. Here is your hope: when Christ unites himself to you, he doesn't leave his grace at the door. He brings to this union all those provisions of grace that you and I need to be what we're supposed to be and to do what we're supposed to do—in sex and in everything else. Your union with Christ welcomes you to be a *sober celebrant*. Sober, because you have grasped the seriousness of your union with Christ, and celebrant, because you understand the hope and help this union provides that can be found no other way.

4. *The Principle of Ownership*

Here is Paul's capstone principle, the principle of ownership: "Do you not know that your body is a temple of the Holy Spirit within you, whom you have from God? You are not your own, for you were bought with a price" (1 Cor. 6:19–20). First, Paul wants every believer to know that grace has claimed your body for a higher purpose than personal, physical pleasure. Your body has been chosen for a higher purpose than anything you could have ever planned or even had the ability to imagine. God Almighty, in the power and glory of his Spirit, has moved in! Now, remember, Paul is reminding you of this in the context of a discussion of the gospel/worship implications on your sexuality. As a believer, whatever you do in your sex life, you do as the temple of the Most High God. Wow! Could there be a more sobering identity concept for the believer to grasp and live out?

The next thing Paul wants you to consider is that, because you are owned by God, the temple of your body does not belong to you anymore. A new landlord has moved in and taken over the management of the building. He has claimed the building for his purposes. No longer a personal pleasure place, the building that is your body has been claimed as a temple for the worship of God alone, and everything you do and all the ways you do it must be done with this new purpose in mind.

Finally, so that you'll take all this seriously in the midst of daily temptation, Paul reminds you of what it cost God to claim you as his own and grace you to be part of something far better than you would have chosen for yourself. The heavy price was the death of his Son. What an insult in the face of that price to act as if you have the right to do whatever you want with your body, whenever you want to do it, and with whomever.

Again, does this high calling defeat and discourage you? Know that what God calls you to, your Savior has already done on your behalf so that in your failure you can run to God rather than from him. Your standing with God is never based on the purity of your heart and hands but on the perfect life of Christ lived for your sake. Confess the places in your sexual life where you think or act as though you own you, and cry out for the forgiving and transforming grace that is yours because your Savior was willing to pay the price.

These four principles are worldview game changers. *Mastery*—your sex life will be shaped by who or what rules your heart. *Eternity*—your sex life will be shaped by whether you live for the temporary pleasures of the here and now or with eternity in view. *Unity*—your sex life will be shaped either by bifurcating your life into the spiritual and secular or by acknowledging that all that makes up you has been united to Christ, and you take Christ wherever you go. *Ownership*—your sex life will be shaped either by acting as if your body belongs to you or by acknowledging that it has been purchased by God for his higher purpose. And your sex life will be shaped either by forgetting the gospel of Jesus Christ preached by each of these principles and hiding in guilt, shame, and fear, or by remembering that Jesus perfectly did all these things so that you, in weakness and failure, would be welcomed into God's presence and receive all the forgiving, transforming, and empowering grace you need to progressively live sexually pure in a world that has gone sexually insane.

Sex and Two Inescapable Worship Commands

Now standing on the foundation of the four sex-and-worship principles we have just examined, Paul leaves us with two simple commands. One is defensive and protective; the other is positive and missional. It is important to note that neither command makes any sense without the worship principles upon which each stands. Each command tells you practically how to live out the personal sexual implications of the identity/worldview that the four principles delineate. This passage, 1 Corinthians 6:12–20, really does have an *indicative* then *imperative* structure. Paul starts by saying, "This is who you are because this is what God has done (the four sex-and-worship principles), so now this is how to live in light of what God has done (the two sex-and-worship commands)."

I cannot adequately express how much I wish I had been exposed to the practical, moral wisdom of this passage as a young man, and I cannot tell you how sad I am presently that this passage isn't taught with more regularity and clarity wherever God's Word is taken seriously.

1. The Command to Flee Sexual Immorality

Here's the bottom line of this defensive and protective command: if you are going to live out the sexual domain of your life in the way that God has called you to live, you are going to have to be willing to do a whole lot of running. You have to be willing to run from thoughts that work to paint as beautiful what God has forbidden. You are going to have to run from desires that at times seem too powerful to resist. You are going to have to run from the seductive whisper of the Enemy, who will lure you with lies. You are going to have to run from situations and locations that play to your weaknesses. You are going to have to run from pride, which tells you that you are stronger than you really are. You are going to have to run from selfishness, which would allow you to use others for your own pleasure. You are going to have to run from things you would love to participate in but would expose you to things you cannot handle. You are simply going to have to run from anything, anywhere, and from any person—all that is immoral in the eyes of your Savior. You have to be willing to run.

Paul's call is not to medieval monasticism. We know that the greatest sexual danger to each of us exists inside, not outside, of us. We know that running won't make us morally pure. But running acknowledges the presence and power of the sin that still lives inside us and how it makes us susceptible to temptation and, sadly, able to see as beautiful and beneficial what God calls ugly and dangerous. As you work to separate yourself from what God names as immoral, you cry out to God to do what you cannot do, that is, to deliver you from you. God calls you to do what he has empowered you by grace to do, as he does for you what you cannot do for yourself. How amazing his grace is!

The question for you is, where in your sexual life do you need to do a better job of running from what God has called and empowered you to run from?

2. The Command to Glorify God in Your Body

Paul ends with the call to live for something bigger than yourself. You have been chosen by God's sovereign grace to live for his glory. Even in the most secret recesses of your private thoughts and desires, you have been chosen to live for his glory. Even in the most naked, private, and intimate activities of your body, you have been chosen to live for his glory. Even in those moments of the most powerful physical and emotional fulfillment, you have been chosen to live for his glory. Even in the most amazing moments of relational connectivity, you have been chosen to live for his glory. Grace has sanctified your whole life, all that makes up you. Grace has set it apart for a greater, higher purpose. Grace has given you new identity, potential, and dignity. Grace has lifted you out of the self-centered mire of the "me-ism" of sin that gives you little purpose greater than the fulfillment of the moment, so that you can live with greater meaning and purpose than you have ever lived with before. Grace gives you back your sanity and your humanity. Grace connects you once again to the purpose for which you were designed and given breath. Grace rescues you from your bondage to passions run wild and thoughts run amok to live in the sanity of God-consciousness that colors your every thought, desire, choice, word, and action. And in so doing, grace introduces you to the highest and most fulfilling pleasures that a human being could ever experience. You see, your greatest pleasures and joys are only ever found in living as you were designed to live, that is, for him.

If sex is about worship, it can't be just about you. "Just about me" sex is sex gone insane. Sex for the glory of the Creator is sex made sane again. Sex as an act of the worship of God is sex made right again. And in this struggle of glory and worship, God meets us with his tender and patient grace. He invites us to confess, believe, and follow and empowers us in every way to live inside of his gracious invitation. So, how are you doing?

Review and Reflect

1. Explain what Paul Tripp means by the "individualization of sex" (p. 102). How has such individualization impacted your life?

2. How does worship factor into sex? Use 1 Corinthians 6:12–20 to guide your answer.

3. Paul Tripp writes, "The principle of mastery is the principle of principles" (p. 105). Describe this principle and why it is vital.

4. How can thinking about your sexuality in light of your union with Christ bring about both fear and hope?

5. Identify the two worship commands Paul Tripp outlines in chapter 7. Are you actively seeking to live out these commands, or do you chronically fail at one or both? If you see little growth in these areas, try to identify wrong beliefs you hold about God or about his Word. As you examine your heart, meditate on Proverbs 18:1.

Heart Reset
- 1 Corinthians 6:12–20

8

If Sex Is about Relationship,
Then It Can't Be Just about You

He had little desire or motivation. If honest, he would have told you that he found her irritating in many ways. He had managed to forge out a schedule and a set of relational rules that meant he could be married but pretty much live on his own, even though they were in the same house. He did all he could to tolerate a civil back-and-forth conversation at the dinner table, but he found most of what she talked about to be incredibly boring. He didn't like her friends and tried to excuse himself from as many of her activities as he could get away with. He controlled their finances and purchases and had the only voice as to how the family was run. He worked hard and provided well, but beyond that, there was little loving in his relationship with his wife.

But despite all the distance and disregard, there was one way he demanded that they connect every day, which was to have sex every evening before sleep. He said it was both his right and God's will. Night after night they had unrelational, unloving sex.

Night after night she did what she was told, even if she found it uncomfortable or embarrassing. Night after night he went to sleep sexually satisfied, and she went to sleep sad and confused and feeling powerless. Night after night she hoped he would fall asleep before demanding sex or just give her one night's break, but it never happened. After giving herself in the most intimate of human activities, he would prepare for work and leave the next morning without even acknowledging her existence. Day after day she dreaded his homecoming because she knew the cycle would begin all over again.

So, what is your response to the sex life of this couple? What would you say to this man? What would you say to his wife? How close is their sexual life to God's intention?

Sex Is Inescapably Relational

There is something deeply disturbing about the sex life of that couple: it isn't really the sex life of a couple; it is the sex life of a man forced upon a woman. At a profound level, though this couple is married, their sex life is a violation of what God designed sex to be. Their sex life is yet another example of the *individualization* of sex. Sex for this man is not an act of love. It is not an act of worshiping God; it is a lifestyle of the pursuit of personal pleasure at the expense of the service and dignity of his wife.

Sex by God's design is meant to occur in the context of two communities of love. Love for God and neighbor is the only location where sex can live according to God's plan. Let me give you the bottom line of this chapter right now: *a living commitment to community protects sex and purifies it from the sin of individualization.* In other words, sex lives with beauty and health only when it grows out of the soil of the two great commands. God, who is himself a community, ordained sex to be an act of community, and when it isn't, it loses its shelter from danger and

destruction. Sex outside of community cannot work as God intended and becomes another example of the insanity that results
from the selfishness of sin. You can't be committed just to having
sex; you also need commitment to the only context in which this
thing you desire was created for. Let's examine the "commitment
to community" context in which God-honoring sex must live.

Sex and Loving God

This may sound a bit weird, but it is true nonetheless: one of the
principal ways human beings love God is in their sexual life. Since
you and I were created to be sexual beings, with sexual desire and
sexual organs, dealing with sex in some way is inescapable. And
since we're created to love God above everything else that exists,
dealing with God in some way is also inescapable. So it is impossible for these two things not to come together in your life. You
will express your sexuality in some way, and you will relate to God
in some way. If you acknowledge that there is no higher, holier call
in all your life than loving God, then you will want everything in
your sexual life to be an expression of that love.

Sex is dangerous when it is motivated only by love of you. Sex is
dangerous when it is motivated only by love for another person. Sex
is dangerous when it is motivated only by love for pleasure. Sex is
dangerous when it is motivated only by love for comfort. Sex is dangerous when it is motivated only by love for control. Sex is dangerous
when it is motivated only by love for sex. Sex is only ever purified
and protected when it is motivated in thought, desire, and action by
a living, submissive, joyful, willing, street-level love for God. Sexual
sin always has a lack of love for God at its core. Or, in other words,
in illicit sex we replace the love we should have for God with love
for something else.

It is always my relationship with God (or lack of it) that shapes
and determines my relationship with you. If I love God as I should,

I will want to relate to you in ways that please and honor him. My love for him will mean that his pleasure trumps my pleasure. It will mean that I have a greater joy in doing his will than in getting my own way. And there will be a joy and a willingness in all this. Perhaps the core character quality of true love is willingness. Love loves to love. Love doesn't see love as a burden or a hassle. Love doesn't love begrudgingly. Love doesn't love kicking and screaming. Love doesn't look for ways of avoiding the call to love. Love doesn't search for ways of escape. Love isn't two-faced and devious. Love is willing and ready to love.

Jesus said it this way: "If you love me, you will keep my commandments" (John 14:15). There is the willingness. Jesus is saying, "If you love me, then you will not see my commands as burdensome. You will not chafe against them. You will willingly and joyfully do what I have told you to do." For most of us, this is very humbling because it requires us to admit what we don't really want to admit. When we are involved in sexual sin (sex outside of God's clear boundaries), we do it because we do not love God as we should. And when God is not in his rightful place, we invariably put ourselves in his position, and we make it all about us. At that point we become self-sovereigns who seek to rule the world for our own pleasure and take as our possession things that do not belong to us.

Let me give you two examples. Think first of the woman lying in bed early in the morning, fantasizing about sex with someone other than her husband. Consider the godlike posture of her fantasy. She is unhappy with the world that actually exists because she did not create it and does not control it, so the real world does not do her bidding or give her what she wants. So in her bed on this morning, she seeks to raise herself to the throne of God and in her mind creates a world as she wants it to be and then rules that world as its absolute sovereign. Everything in her self-created world is her possession, and everything in her world submits to her pleasure. She is attracted to this world because in it she is creator and lord. So she sets the rules. She uses what she has created as she wants to use it and for whatever pleasure she seeks. And she'll visit this world again because she finds it way more attractive than the world that really exists.

The man she has taken for her pleasure in her fantasy does not belong to her, and the things she has dreamed of doing with him are not her right to do. She has removed God from her universe, taken his throne, possessed what belongs to him, thrown away his rules, and written a new set. The whole thing is an outrageous violation of the loving community she was created to have with God, which would then shape every thought, desire, choice, and action in her life. Her problem isn't first that she loves herself too much or fails to love the man she has objectified in her fantasy. The problem is even greater and way more serious than a failure to love God. In her fantasy, even if just for a moment, she has killed God, taken his position, re-created the world as a garden for her own pleasure, and used it as she and she alone wills. What she is doing in her bed is not a little thing. It is a horrible thing, and each time she does it, it will make it harder for her to accept the real world, where she doesn't have the position of God. In the real world she will be more and more tempted to act as the sovereign that she isn't and to attempt to possess and experience what does not belong to her. Her fantasy is the portal to greater sexual insanity, but she doesn't know it. In fact, she prides herself on not acting upon the dreams she has been able to conjure up.

Something beautiful, purifying, and protective is missing in her heart. It is something that God intended to be the core motivator of every person he created. What is it? It is willing, joyful, submissive, and active rubber-meets-the-road love for him. It is the only thing that will ever produce sexual purity. Sexual purity begins in the heart with a love for God that overwhelms all the other loves that battle for the allegiance of the heart.

Or consider this second example. A man is walking home from work and lusting after the woman approaching him on the sidewalk. He slows down his walk to get a longer look, and he turns around and watches as she passes. Think with me again about the godlike posture of the man. First, he is treating this moment as if it belongs to him. It's as if he is sovereign and she is on the sidewalk according to his will and for his pleasure. He is owning the moment as his own. This location is his location, there to bring him the pleasure he sees as his right. He's the self-appointed deity of the moment. He thinks of no other God and worships no one but himself. The world has shrunk to the size of his desire, and he rules it for his pleasure. He doesn't give a rip at that moment about right or wrong, because there is for that moment no higher authority than himself. He will have what he will have, even if it is only the right to stare at body parts and imagine having them for his pleasure.

But there is more. For that moment he is stealing God's creation and taking it as his own. He has no right to this woman. She does not actually belong to him in any way, but he takes her with his eyes and his mind. He tries to slow down the moment in order to enjoy his sexual thievery for as long as he can. He's ripped this woman out of the hands of God and claimed her as his own for whatever momentary pleasure he can achieve. She feels his eyes and is uncomfortable. She wants to get away, but she has to walk by. She feels a bit violated, but it's not the first time. She's walked by this guy and other guys like him before.

In that moment this man is the fool. He has denied God's existence. He has set himself up as God. He has robbed God of his creation. He has thrown God off his throne. He has a much deeper problem than his wandering eyes and fickle affections. He has become comfortable dethroning God and possessing what does not belong to him, and if he continues to do it with his mind, he will begin to do it with his hands. Remember, lust does not lust for more lust. Lust lusts for the actual thing, the real experience. He is in danger because his heart has become comfortable with what by God's design is a horrible, unnatural thing—a life-shaping, danger-exposing lack of love for God.

Recognition of and living for the community with God for which I was created keeps my sexual life pure. There is simply no other way. Heart-controlling love for God protects my heart from wandering to all the places it could wander in this sexually insane world.

As you read this, what are you thinking? I'll tell you what I have been thinking. I have had to face the sad truth that I dethrone God all the time. I view the world as mine again and again. It is the tragedy of remaining sin. There are ways in which I still want God's throne, and desire to claim as mine what belongs to him. Perhaps it is in a moment of lust on the street, or an impatient word to someone who's made me wait, or envying what someone else has. As I have written, I have been forced to acknowledge that I am not free from the struggles about which I am writing. I am still capable of being that God-denying fool. To my grief I must confess that there are times when I think I am smarter than God, that my rule would be better than his. To my grief I must face the fact that this never, ever leads anywhere good.

Does this mean that I am without hope? How could it be, with all I know and all I've experienced as God's child, that these struggles still exist? Sure, there are times when I get it right and my heart is filled with love and gratitude for God, but not always. In the face of the acknowledgment of my fickle heart, my hope still remains firm and secure. Why? Because my security has never been in the degree of my love for God but in the unshakable and eternal character of his love for me. And as I come to him in poverty of spirit, not only will he not turn me away; he will greet me with open arms and the lavish provision of his right-here, right-now grace. His transforming love remains faithful even when mine doesn't. He will not abandon the promises of his grace, even when I don't value them as I should. He will not quit being my Lord in those moments when I would rather be my own lord. He will not fold up his kingdom and go home when I would rather construct a kingdom of my own that does my bidding. Yes, he will chasten me with his hands of fatherly grace, but he will not throw me out of his family and abandon the work in me and for me that he has begun.

So I run to him and confess that sex isn't my problem; vertical love is. I confess that sex is where my ongoing temptation to dethrone God is revealed, controls my world, and writes my own rules for my selfish purpose and pleasure. Again, I kneel before him, confessing the disloyalty of my heart, seeking the grace that is my only hope of purity of heart and hands. I pray again that he would give me the heart to love willingly and consistently until the struggle to love is no more. And I pray that this living and active love for him would overwhelm any love I have for something in the creation that battles for the affection of my heart.

These prayers are significant not only for me but for you too, because the struggle for sexual purity is really a struggle to keep God in his rightful place in your heart—at the center of your affections and motivations.

Sex and Loving Your Neighbor

Sex is also purified and protected by a second community of love, love for your neighbor. Illicit sex never treats another as an object of affection. Illicit sex is never motivated and shaped by self-sacrificing love for another. Illicit sex never wants what is good for another. Illicit sex doesn't willingly submit to another's needs. Illicit sex doesn't answer the higher call to be part of what God is doing in another's life. Illicit sex always replaces relational love with entitled, demanding, selfish, personal pleasure. Illicit sex is all about me to the detriment of you. Illicit sex objectifies and dehumanizes another. You become to me less than God's image bearer. You are reduced to little more than an object for my momentary sexual pleasure. Illicit sex denies the Second Great Commandment, uproots sex from its God-intended community and plants it in the world of individual pleasure, where it was never meant to germinate and grow.

One of the horrific things about pornography is the way in which it is fundamentally antirelational. Sex is reduced to graphic fantasies, sexual activities, and sexual climax. There is not even a consideration of relationship, let alone committed marital love. The man and the woman are together not as an expression of anything remotely relational but because they want sexual pleasure. So rather than expressing affection of any kind, the sex they engage in is just a personal pursuit of sex. The man uses the body of the woman, and the woman uses the body of the man. It's sex for sex's sake or sex for money's sake, but it is not sex for love's sake, because there is no love needed when all you are trying to do is use the body of the other to reach physical sexual climax. Pornographic videos tend not to be love stories.

One of the horrible things about sex in advertising is that it is fundamentally antirelational. The body of a woman is used to sell an automobile, for instance. Now, think about this. The advertiser intentionally plays to the sexual desires of male consumers, using the sexuality of the woman to attract the attention of the potential buyer. He tries to create a connection between the sex appeal of the woman and the sex appeal of the car. He doesn't care if the man buys the car as a "sex" decision rather than as a sound financial decision as long as he buys the car. The woman in the ad is reduced to something less than human. She is not respected for her mind, her character, and her gifts. She is not esteemed and loved. It is her sexuality that you notice, her body that you desire. Sadly, in the ad, the woman, who is made in the image of God, is reduced to the level of the car—a sexy object designed to bring you pleasure. The intentionality and methodology of the commercial is a denial of the Second Great Commandment. Illicit sex always denies this command because it is not interested in relationship. It's interested only in personal sexual pleasure.

God's design is that sex would only ever take place in the context of a committed, lifelong relationship between a man and a woman in marriage. Sex is protected and purified by this commitment to tender, faithful, self-sacrificing, other-serving love. In this context I am not after my own pleasure and using you to get it. In this context, even in my most intimate, physical, and exciting connection to you, I am loving you and looking out for your welfare. The way I relate to you and touch you and the things we do in sex are all then guided and directed by relational love, not just sexual excitement.

Now, I think this helps us understand why there is so much sexual dysfunction even in the lives of married couples. I am convinced that usually the problem isn't that couples are ignorant of the structure and function of their bodies. As I've written before, I don't think we need a bunch of new Christian "body part" books. Look, most of us know where stuff is on the body, and we know how things were made to function. Little of this dysfunction is the result of ignorance. Here's what the problem is: you will always drag the character and quality of your marriage relationship into the marriage bed because sex is fundamentally relational.

To deny that sex is a relationship is just insanity. If I have nourished you and cherished you, if I have been willing to serve you, if

I have been giving, forgiving, forbearing, kind, gentle, patient, and respectful of you in our everyday relationship, then in this moment where there is no protection, where you are literally naked next to me in the most vulnerable of human moments, you will know that you can trust me to love you, and you can relax, naked in my arms. But if I have been critical, entitled, and demanding, if I have been unforgiving and bitter, if I have been impatient, rude, selfish, and unkind, in this moment where you are naked next to me, you will not feel safe. You will fear that the unkind things you have experienced with me relationally, you will now experience also in sex. You will fear being used and criticized rather than loved and nurtured. And because you are afraid, you'll find it hard to give yourself in the way you must in order for sex to work as God intended.

Most sexually dysfunctional couples don't need sex education as much as they need relational confession and reconciliation. Because God designed sex to be experienced in the context of relationship and as an expression of that relationship, you can't escape the nature of your relationship to your husband or wife when you are having sex. It simply isn't possible. These dysfunctional couples are trying to find sexual pleasure outside of a commitment to the kind of relationship God has called them to have. And even though they are having marital sex, they have little commitment to the relationship of love that is meant to be the context for this intimate act, and therefore, at the level of their hearts, they are in violation of God's plan. Unloving, demanding sex experienced apart from the context of living, active, relational love simply isn't God-honoring sex.

Let me take this discussion further. I understand why so many men struggle with Internet pornography. If sex, for you, has not been an act of relational love, if you have essentially used the body of your wife for your own selfish sexual pleasure, if your wife has been reduced to a means of your getting off, then it makes sense that you would be very tempted to replace her with digital images and selfish fantasies that accomplish the same thing. There are marriages in which men are sexually unkind to their wife, sexually demanding, sexually selfish, and sexually critical. They are much more interested in their wife's sexually performing for them than they are committed to loving their wife sexually. They have little interest in the comfort and pleasure of their wife. They demand things that make their wife uncomfortable and instill guilt in the face of their wife's protests. The sex in their marriage doesn't look like love. It looks like the self-sovereign, my-pleasure-first individualization of sex that is everywhere in the surrounding culture. Shockingly, they use the wife's marriage vows as a tool to get her to submit to whatever selfish sexual demands they make, all the while claiming that it is their right. Perhaps without understanding what they are doing, they have denigrated marital sex, bringing it down to a level just above masturbation, and they have reduced their wife to a machine for their own pleasure. This kind of sex life meets none of the requirements to love God or to love neighbor and is therefore horrible in the eyes of God.

Because the marital sex life of these men has been more masturbatory than relational, it makes sense that they have little defense against the readily available pornography that offers them the selfish pleasure they seek without the burden of having to relate to another in the process. They easily matriculate from one kind of antirelational sex to another with none of the love commitments of heart that would protect them and reveal pornography as the horror it actually is. It is sad that so much of this is going on in the church and maybe even sadder that no one is talking about it.

Sex in marriage isn't made holy simply because it's in marriage, anymore than talk in marriage is made holy because it's in marriage. Both sex and talk are made holy by the intentions of your heart, and the intentions are holy when by powerful transforming grace you love God above all else and your neighbor as yourself.

Part of the insanity of human culture when it comes to sex is our ability to philosophically or practically deny its God-ordained relational context. You can do this inside or outside of marriage. Yes, according to God's design only married couples are free to have sex, but just because you're married, it doesn't necessarily follow that your sex life is an expression of the two Great Commandments.

This is why Jesus willingly went to the cross, so that "those who live might no longer live for themselves" (2 Cor. 5:15), no longer for divine dethronement. Jesus died to dethrone you and to enthrone God in your heart. Now in that there is hope, not only for your sex life but for everything else in your life as well.

Review and Reflect

1. Explain why Paul Tripp writes that "a living commitment to community protects sex and purifies it from the sin of individualization" (p. 120).

2. Describe what makes sex dangerous.

3. In what ways is illicit sex antithetical to real love? How does our society mask this reality?

4. What impact does illicit sex have on marital relationships? Conversely, how does a biblically grounded sex life enable a marriage to flourish?

5. Paul Tripp has found hope in personal failure because he roots his security not in his love for God but in "the unshakable and eternal character" of God's love for him (pp. 125–26). Reread that entire section of chapter 8 and then determine where and how you might apply it to yourself.

Heart Reset

- John 14:15–17

- 2 Corinthians 5:14–15

9

If Sex Is about Obedience, Then It Can't Be Just about You

I tell parents all the time that one of the first and most important heart issues for young children is authority. Sinners naturally dislike authority. They tend to want to be their own authority. Sinners are oriented to self-sovereignty and the writing of their own moral code. Children tend not to ask their parents for more rules and closer accountability. Children tend not to celebrate when they have been told what to do. Children tend to look at authority as something that robs them of freedom. Children tend not to see authority as a blessing. Natural rebellion to authority, which in some way is the state of all sinners, is one of the principal heart struggles for every human being.

All this is important because you will never deal with the sex issue until you have first dealt with the authority issue. As we've noted throughout, the sexual struggle and the sexual insanity of the culture are rooted in something deeper than sex. They are rooted in a rejection of the authority of God over every area of human existence. They are rooted in a deep desire for self-rule.

They are rooted in the human drive to take charge of one's own life. They are rooted in the deep and abiding cultural heresy that says, "My body belongs to me and no one has the right to tell me what to do with it." The sexual insanity all around us is, in fact, anti-authority madness that cannot and will not go anywhere good, because it violates the very nature of who we are and how the world was designed to operate.

As we've already seen, little children and grown men and women alike need to be confronted with the stark reality that it will never be about them, because they have been born into a world that by its very nature is the celebration of another. They have been born into a world not owned by them. They have been born into a world that was not intended to be ruled by them. Any authority humans have is representative or ambassadorial. Human authority is never ultimate. Every human authority is placed where it has been placed to visibly represent the invisible authority of God. Here is the bottom line that must then shape the way you view everything, including sex: the world we live in is a world under rule. This means that I do not have the right to do whatever I want to do, whenever, however, and with whomever I want to do it. Because there is an authority over all things, there is law. And because there is law, for every area of my life, there are morally right things to do and morally wrong things.

So the issue for every human being is, will I submit to the directives of the One who rules over all, or will I deny his authority and write my own rules? This is the ultimate and inescapable human decision. So sex can't be just about reaching the highest moment of pleasure, because that is an essentially lawless way of looking at sex. Sex has to be about obedience to the law. If there is an authority who rules every dimension of your life, then sex can't be just about you. It is always about God's will, his way, his plan, his pleasure, and his glory and about the degree of your willingness to submit to him.

Another factor is the lie of self-sufficiency. This lie tells me that I have everything I need inside of me to be what I'm supposed to be and to do what I'm supposed to do. I do not need the help, wisdom, and guidance of another. I am able to figure it all out, and I am able to live the kind of life I was designed to live with no outside assistance. The fact is really the opposite. Human beings were not created to live independently or self-sufficiently. Human beings were created to be dependent. We were created with fundamental needs that we cannot meet on our own. We are born with a need for a wisdom we don't have. We are born with a need for strength we do not possess. We all need to be taught and enabled and, because of sin, rescued and transformed. The self-made person is a fantasy. The independent human being is a delusion. We are weak and needy, all of us. There simply is no escaping it.

So this is the way I should view myself, including my sexual self. In sex I will either accept the fact that I am weak and needy and seek the help of my Creator or deny the empirical evidence I daily give of who I am and act as if I know what I do not know and am able to do what I cannot do. So armed with a belief that my body is mine to use as I choose and that I am wise and strong, I will write my own sex manual and do what I want with my body and the bodies of others, all the while telling myself that I am wise and that what I am doing is good. And day after day I will deny my sexual insanity and blame on others the trouble that results.

It bears repeating that the sexual mess all around us is much, much more than a sex mess. It is a mess of self-worship, a denial of community, a rejection of authority, and the individualization of sex that results. You cannot move toward sexual sanity without addressing these root issues. You can't isolate sex and successfully fix sex without dealing with the underlying issues that have caused the mess to be the mess that it is.

The little child who becomes comfortable rejecting the authority of God, as it comes through the authority of his parents, is heading for sexual insanity. The teenage girl who mocks her parents as hyperconservative and embarrassingly old-fashioned, and so rejects their authority, is heading for sexual insanity. The college graduate who has been persuaded that his life is his for the using is headed for sexual insanity. The middle-aged man who thinks he has the independent strength to keep his sexual desires in check is headed for sexual insanity. There is no escaping it—your sex life always reveals how you are dealing with the unavoidable issue of authority. You submit to the laws of the King, or you set yourself up as king. That's it; there is no neutral world to live in.

What Does Obedience Look Like?

Obedience is more than a set of behaviors; obedience is an attitude of the heart. I will pirate the definition that my brother, Tedd, has given for obedience: *Obedience is the willing submission of my heart to God that causes me to do what God has commanded without challenge, excuse, or delay.* May I say at the get-go that an obedient heart protects and purifies your sex life. At the core of sexual purity lives a willing recognition of and submission to the authority of God.

Let's unpack Tedd's definition. The essence of obedience is not simply doing the right stuff. Rather, the essence of obedience is the heart, and what must live in the heart of the obedient person is a willing submission to God's authority. Obedience that is not willingly submissive is not obedience. If you must force, cajole, threaten, or guilt others into obedience, you have to do that precisely because they are not obedient. They lack the willingness that is at the center of every obedient life. Sexually pure people are pure because they have a willing heart, and because they have a willing heart, they are ready to say no to powerful desires, raging emotions, and seductive temptations, turning and doing what God has called them to do. The person who fights what is right, who constantly questions it, who looks for ways around it, and who occasionally even mocks it will not be sexually pure for very long because he does not carry around within him an obedient heart. He will not be able to stand against the daily temptations he will face in this world gone sexually insane, and he will not say no to his quickly wandering desires.

This willingness of heart causes me to have a "what-has-God-commanded?" way of looking at my life. I don't mean that I live a legalistic, rules-bound existence or that I live tentatively and fearfully. I am saying that I have a *boundaries* way of thinking about life. If God is in charge, and if he has decided what is morally right and wrong, and if he has clearly communicated that to me, then there are moral boundaries of heart and behavior inside of which I am called to live. Inside those boundaries is a life of beautiful freedom and happiness. Outside those boundaries are danger, destruction, and death.

Think of the word picture of boundaries. Pretend you are living in a yard that contains every good, true, and beautiful thing a human being could ever want, and around the yard is a twenty-foot-high chain-link fence. And consider further that outside, on the other side of the fence, is a world of real danger, full of things that will cause your death. If you accepted that what is inside the yard is really very good—things that give you life—and if you accepted that what is outside the fence is really very bad—things that lead to death—wouldn't you be thankful for the fence? And wouldn't you be willing to live inside the fence with contentment and joy?

But think with me: if you looked at that fence every day, thinking about how you could get through it or over it, if you touched it or shook it to test its strength, if you tried your best to look through it until you had fence marks on your face, wouldn't you be doing all that because you believe that the good stuff may be on the other side of the fence? You see, you have much more than a behavior problem; you have a boundary problem. You don't believe that the fence is there to ensure that you have what is good. No, you have come to believe that the fence is in the way of good, and the minute you allow yourself to believe that, you are on your way to finding a means of getting to the other side of the fence.

In my sexual life I am willing to submit to God's commands because, deep within my heart, I really do think they are good. I really do believe that God's laws give life and freedom; they don't rob me of it. I really do believe that God is wise, good, and trustworthy. I really do think that it is best to live inside his boundaries. So I willingly, in my heart and with my hands, do what God has commanded me to do with my sexual self. I'm not staring at the fence wondering if the good sexual stuff lives out there. I am not haunted by thoughts of what I am missing. I am not unhealthily curious about the lives and sexual exploits of people on the other side of the fence. And I don't feel disadvantaged because I've been chosen to live inside the fence. Rather, I turn my back to the fence and joyfully celebrate all the rich and good things I've been given that I would never have had the sense to choose for myself. I wake up each morning feeling not restricted but blessed, and I surely don't equate freedom with having my own way. I know I need fences in every area of my life, including sex, and I know that without God's boundaries I would wander into dangers that would be my doom. God's boundaries do not inhibit a joyful sexual life; they are the only context in which it can be fully experienced.

Now, back to our definition. The qualifiers in the definition are important: "without challenge." If in my heart I am yelling at God because he won't allow me to do what I want to do, if I am questioning whether he is good and kind, if I am mad because I can't do what others seem free to do, I do not have an obedient heart. The heart of an obedient person does what is right but doesn't kick and scream all the way. Obedient people are not angry at God as they are obeying. You're not actually submissive to God in your sexual life if you're mad at him for what he has told you not to do. You're not obedient to God in sex if you're questioning God's character and wisdom. You don't have an obedient heart in your sex life if you often wish that the world was ruled by someone else who would give you more freedom. Sexual purity begins with resting assured that what God commands is kind, wise, and good; no need for challenge.

The second qualifier is equally important: "without . . . excuse." An obedient person doesn't excuse his sexual sin; he mourns it. We are never more creative than when manufacturing "logical" reasons for stepping beyond God's loving, protective, and clear boundaries. We don't want to face the fact that at some point we are all fools and rebels. We want to think of ourselves as wise, reasonable, and moral. So we work to convince ourselves, others, and maybe even God that what we have done is not so bad after all, because look at what we were dealing with or facing. We may even try to convince ourselves that there was no other way, that what looked foolish was really smart, or that it's not so bad just this once. If you can convince yourself that it's right, even good, to live on the other side of God's boundaries, you're heading for sexual insanity of some kind. You will hop God's fences and do with your body and the body of another what you should not do, all the while convincing yourself that it is okay.

The third qualifier is even more deceptive: "without . . . delay." The obedient heart is quickly willing. If you are willingly submitting to God, you do it right away and without delay. You don't say, "I'll start obeying God in my sex life tomorrow." Delay is just one of many ways we seek to retain our autonomy and self-sovereignty. Here's how delay operates:

> You're flirting with a woman at work, and it has become a bit sexual. You know you shouldn't be doing it, but you sit down with her again in the lunchroom and tell yourself that you'll cut it off tomorrow.

> Your heart is pounding as you're surfing toward that porn site, hoping your wife doesn't wake up. You know you have no business being there, but to ease your guilt you tell yourself this is the last time.

> You're seventeen, and you're in the local park at night with your girlfriend. You've got your hand inside her bra. Your hand is shaking with a combination of excitement and fear. You know that what you're doing is wrong for you and for her, but you couldn't resist one more time. You tell yourself you'll break it off with her in the next few days.

> You're living with a woman who is not your wife, and you've recently committed yourself to Christ. You know you should not be sleeping with your girlfriend, but you tell yourself it will be such a hassle to separate and find separate apartments. You'll deal with it, but you can't handle it right now.

> You know you've gotten hooked on a television series you have no business watching. It leaves you thinking in impure ways, but you tell yourself that you'll finish out the season and not watch the new season in the fall.

Delay is disobedience in a tuxedo. Delay gives you room to rebel against the authority of God while telling yourself that you have every intention to obey, and in so doing you've eased your conscience when it actually needs to be troubled. Your sex life is always a window on how your heart is responding to the inescapable authority of God.

Sex and Disobedience

It's important to understand that, like obedience, disobedience is not just a set of behaviors; it's first a condition of the heart. So it's important to understand the psychology or posture of the heart behind obedience.

Part of the psychology of disobedience is to somehow, someway, convince yourself that you're smarter than God. Your rules are better or more practical than his rules. Your desires are more legitimate than those he desires for you. What you've planned for yourself is better than what he has willed for you. Maybe it's just telling yourself that the sexual boundary you're stepping over isn't such a big deal just this once. Or it doesn't make sense that you can't sleep with someone you love even if you aren't married. Or you reason that culture has evolved, that we know things we didn't know when the Bible was written; it doesn't make any sense to be controlled by outdated, culturally bound rules. Disobedience always involves placing more reliability and value on your wisdom than on God's. You make a choice to do what makes sense or appears attractive, regardless of what God has said on the topic. Your position, when it comes to the wisdom of God, is not one of submission; it is one of critique. Whether or not you know it, you're standing above God, willing to reject what comes from him, what makes no sense to you.

Disobedience not only claims greater wisdom; it claims ownership. You find doing what you want to do comfortable because you view your life as belonging to you. If your life belongs to you, then you are entitled to do with it what you want. Disobedience always has an ownership posture. It claims rights that no human being has. As we laid out in a previous chapter, God owns you and everything about you. Any posture of ownership is a delusion that will only expose you to danger. You don't have a right to your own body, because your body doesn't belong to you. Disobedience also requires your willingness to reject the moral law of God and write your own moral code. It gives you the authority to determine what is right and wrong, good or bad, true or false. But this is an authority that only God has. One of the sweetest graces in the Old Testament is when God, who knows everything from origin to destiny, tells his newly re-deemed people how he's created them to live. He did not design them to be morally self-guiding; he lovingly gives them the moral guidance they desperately need. You are always submitting to God's law, or you're writing your own laws.

Finally, disobedience involves easing your conscience by argu-ing all the time for the logic of what you're doing. You are able to be comfortable with stepping over God's boundaries because you are a very committed and skilled self-swindler. We all do it. We tell ourselves that we're the good guys, that what we're doing isn't really that bad, and that our little sins aren't technically sins at all. Self-swindling works to quiet your internal restraint system that tells you to say no when you want to say yes. Self-swindling works to dull the pain of a conscience that is under the conviction of the Holy Spirit. Self-swindling is selling to yourself that you can be disobedient and still retain your allegiance to God.

I remember being a bit stunned in a moment of counseling when an unfaithful and adulterous man said to me, "You would understand what I did [speaking of his sexual relationship with another woman] if you lived with my wife." It was the old "my wife made me do it" argument. He was saying in desperation that he'd been driven to this act by the horrible woman he was forced to live with. This is what self-swindling does. It rejects personal responsibility and all the moral choices of the heart that always lie behind doing what is wrong in the eyes of God, and it works to make us feel good about what God clearly says is not good.

Jesus Wants Your Body

Sex is never just about physical pleasure. Sex is never just about horizontal relationships. Sex is always about obedience. Your sex life is shaped either by a willing submission to the authority of God or by you taking authority over your life and body as if it belongs to you. There is no escape.

This issue of obedience extends to the most intimate uses of your body. It is here that Romans 12:1 is very helpful: "I appeal to you therefore brothers, by the mercies of God, to present your bodies as a living sacrifice, holy and acceptable to God, which is your spiritual worship." It could not be stated more clearly and eloquently. This passage connects your body to worship and obedience. Worship of God means you willingly give your body to him. You forever forsake ownership of your body and what you do with it. You view your body as belonging to God—his for the using. And you commit yourself to an obedient use of your body, that is, to doing with your body only what is holy and acceptable in his sight, no matter what your passions, thoughts, or desires tell you. Sexual purity is found in the intentional sacrifice of your body to God—no longer your desire and your way, but according to his will and for his glory.

And it's important to understand that the directive in Romans 12:1 is not God's way of robbing you of life simply because he is in charge and has the power. Paul puts all this in the context of God's mercy. This is grace. In calling us to make this intentional bodily sacrifice, God is rescuing us from us and protecting us from the dangers of a world gone mad. And all this reminds us that we need God's law, but we must understand its limits. God's law is effective in exposing our moral neediness; it works to give us moral tracks to run on, but it cannot transform us. The law has no ability to make our hearts willing and pure. If it could, the Redeemer, Christ Jesus, wouldn't have had to come to live and die and rise again in our place.

So sexual purity doesn't begin with a commitment to keep God's law; it begins with a confession that you don't want to and you can't. It requires the confession of the selfishness and rebellion of your heart. It owns that you often find impurity more attractive than purity. You see, if sexual impurity was just a matter of a wrong set of behaviors, then the move toward purity would be just a matter of replacing old behaviors with new and better ones. If sexual impurity were just a matter of the lust of the heart, then that would be the thing you would need to address. But the reality is that sexual impurity is rooted in things that are vastly deeper than wrong thoughts and wrong actions. Sexual impurity grows in the soil of the scary condition of the sinful heart. I struggle with sexual impurity in the same way I struggle with materialism or gluttony, because I struggle with something deeper. What is this deeper thing? I struggle with self-worship and self-rule. In my heart there are still ways in which I want to be at the center of my world, where what I want, feel, or think I need is more important to me than God's will or the real needs of those around me. There are ways in which I am so busy loving and worshiping me that I have little time or energy left to love God or others.

I grapple every day with self-worship, and because I do, I want to be sovereign over my own life. I want to rule my life and set up my own rules. I want to have what seems best to me, and I don't want God or others to get in the way. I cannot escape how sex exposes both of these things in my heart. My sex life is always shaped by who I worship and by whose rules I submit to.

So when I face the deeper struggle of sexual purity, I am not helped just by getting a greater understanding of my sexual self, a clearer awareness of where I am susceptible to temptation, or a better system of accountability. Those things are helpful, but they easily become a way of asking the law to do what only grace can accomplish. My struggle with sexual purity reveals the degree to which I still need a fundamental renewal or transformation of my heart. It is only when I worship God above everything else, love my neighbor as myself, and willingly submit to God's authority that I will be pure. In the most basic sense, when it comes to the sexual purity battle, I have met the enemy, and it is me. I am the greatest sexual danger to me. I am my greatest source of temptation. I am the source of my struggle. The self-worship and self-sovereignty that still live in my heart cause me to be attracted and susceptible to the sexual temptations everywhere around me in this world that has gone sexually insane.

So does this leave me hopeless? No! God, who knows how deep my struggle is, has gifted me with the lavish provisions of his powerful rescuing and transforming grace.

Where does purity start? It starts by confessing your profound need and that you are unable to change what needs to be changed. Sexual purity doesn't begin with setting up a regimen for behavioral change. It begins with mourning the condition of your heart, and when you do, you can rest assured that you will be greeted with powerful grace because your Savior has promised that he will never turn his back when you come to him with a broken and contrite heart.

Without this deeper heart confession, behavioral reformation and community accountability won't ultimately free you.

Review and Reflect

1. Why do human beings struggle to submit to God's authority? How does self-sufficiency factor into our struggle with authority?

2. Chapter 9 contains a definition for *obedience*: "Obedience is the willing submission of my heart to God that causes me to do what God has commanded without challenge, excuse, or delay" (p. 136). As you consider your sex life in light of this definition, where do you see misalignment? Identify specific thoughts, words, or deeds.

3. Describe the ways in which a submissive heart nourishes the ability to live within biblical boundaries.

4. Explain how the "psychology of disobedience" works (p. 141). Where have you seen this play out in your own life and choices? Take into account what you identified in question 2 above.

5. Paul Tripp writes, "An obedient person doesn't excuse his sexual sin; he mourns it" (p. 139). How does Psalm 32 reveal the constructive way to deal with sin? Name specific steps shown in the psalm.

Heart Reset
- Romans 12:1–2

10

So Where Do We Go from Here?

It was hard for him to remember when sex hadn't been a struggle. It was hard to remember a day when he hadn't been hit with guilt, shame, regret, and fear. It was hard for him to remember what it was like to feel free and normal. It was hard for him.

The world of sex had been opened up to him long before he was emotionally or spiritually mature enough to handle it. In middle school he fell in with a group of boys who shared sex as their common interest. They knew little more than that women's bodies were different and interesting and well worth investigating. Their conversations were dirty and uninformed, but they were compelling. He found himself thinking about women's "parts" and about how to get the girls at school to show him stuff. It wasn't long before he was stealing men's magazines from the local drug store and hanging around the women's dressing rooms at the local department store.

His thoughts about hanging out with girls had little to do with relationship. He was on a constant search for the girls who would "put out," although he would've denied it if you had accused him. In high school he became increasingly obsessed with and addicted to sex. In it he found identity, power, and pleasure that he could find nowhere else. He had a stash of paper and video pornography hidden at home and was always on the prowl outside his home, but his parents had no idea. To them, his interest in girls was just a teenage boy being a teenage boy.

His first three years of college were made up of mandatory classes and a whole lot of drinking and sex. If not with a female college classmate, he spent the weekend at local strip clubs. He had no idea of the deep emotional and spiritual trouble he was in. He had no concept of the damage he was doing to his soul. In his fourth year of college he was invited to a party by a girl he thought was pretty hot, so he gladly accepted the invitation. What he didn't know was that the party was sponsored by a campus ministry. It didn't seem like much of a party, but he continued to accept the girl's invitations to these ministry gatherings because he was interested in her and intrigued by what he heard. Although he wasn't able to describe it, he was increasingly concerned about himself and how he was living. He felt guilt and regret as he had never experienced in his life. He began to ask questions of the people in charge, and before long he had given his heart to the Lord.

Although on one hand he was filled with joy, on the other hand he felt as if he carried a heavy burden around with him every day. He knew he was God's child, and he knew he was forgiven, but he also soon knew that he wasn't free of sexual temptation. There were times when he missed the old days and desperately wanted what he knew he couldn't have. But he didn't think it was possible to tell his Christian friends about his struggle. What would they think of him? What would they do? He decided there was no way to share with others his addiction. He would give himself to knowing his faith and trying better. He would get involved in all the activities he could, and he would hang with the right people. He would read his Bible every morning and focus on the right things throughout the day. He was on God's side, and he would kick this thing.

But he didn't kick it; it recaptured him. It started with titillating sites on the Internet, then increased secret viewing of pornography and sneaking out to the occasional strip club. He felt scared and defeated but would not reach out for help; there just seemed to be no way. In the midst of this, there were ways in which he did grow and his life did change. He grew in biblical literacy and theological understanding. He involved himself in the ministries of the campus church. As his heart was being torn in two different directions, he met his future wife. She was beautiful, pure, and spiritually mature. She seemed almost too good to be true. For him, it was as close as one could get to love at first sight, but it also made him afraid. What if she knew who he really was? What if she knew where he had been and what he had done? What if she ever found him looking at pornography—then what?

He decided two things. First, there was no way he was going to jeopardize the first good relationship of his life by telling her things she simply couldn't handle. He would never open up. He would avoid the need to answer direct questions. He would hide his struggle. Second, he determined that illicit sex was gone, in his past, never to return. And he knew how he would pull it off— marriage. Clearly, God had brought her into his life to help him defeat something he hadn't been able to defeat. The legitimate sexual relationship of marriage would liberate him from his desire to have illegitimate sex outside of marriage. He was so happy. He proposed, she accepted, and they married two months after graduation.

The first several months of marriage made him feel free from the struggles of his past. The newness, freedom, and excitement of sex with his wife in the context of marriage kept his thoughts and desires focused. He began to think that he had turned the corner, that is, until that day at the mall. Not only did he notice that attractive woman and think things he hadn't thought in a while, but also he followed her around, hoping to see more. He left the mall devastated but still not willing to tell his secret. The next several years were a great struggle mixed with occasional times of freedom. But the draw was getting stronger, and he was living a double life. His wife had little idea or concern. The only thing that bothered her was that they didn't have sex as often as they once had. He knew he was in trouble, but for all his belief in God's power, he didn't have much hope.

- - -

She had been the cheerleader, prom queen, and all-around golden girl, but by her own admission and in her own words she had been a slut. She loved to be the tease. She loved the power of seduction. She loved hearing guys beg. She loved dressing a bit provocatively, and she loved being noticed. She loved having the body that men wanted to touch. She loved being the center of attention, and if sex was the way to get to the center, then so be it.

High school was all about being the girl everyone wanted or wanted to be. It was all about sexually teasing her male classmates and making out in the car with a selected few. She liked her body and the fact that men liked it too, and she grew more and more comfortable with using her body to get what she wanted. It all seemed to be the life of her dreams until the end of college. She wanted to get married but had little idea that marriage would be the end of the lifestyle that got her up in the morning and kept her going.

Once she had the man, the pattern of tease, conquest, and seduction was over. Sex for her had not been an expression of commitment and love. It had been about personal power and pleasure.

So she found sex in marriage neither exciting nor attractive. Sure, it was exciting at first, but it soon became mundane and boring. She found herself flirting at work or in the grocery store. It was wrong, but it was exciting. She employed the double meaning, stood closer to men than she should, and dressed to get attention. More and more she felt trapped by her marriage. More and more she was distant from her husband. And that day when she kissed her fellow worker in the stockroom, she knew she was in trouble. The problem was that she didn't know what to do. She wanted what she could not have and didn't want what she had been given. And on top of it all, she was convinced that if she was honest about her past and her present struggle, she would lose everything. She decided to keep silent and to quit messing around, but her feelings and the temptations didn't go away.

The Gospel of Jesus Christ and Sex

Perhaps these stories touch your story or perhaps not. The fact is that many Christians are in the midst of some kind of personal sexual struggle or dysfunction. There are many married couples in the church who do not experience the beautiful, intimate sexual oneness that God designed. There are many professing Christian men living a double life. There are many Christian singles succumbing to temptations they are called to fight. There are many Christians whose minds wander daily and whose desires regularly go astray. And many of these brothers and sisters in the faith live in fearful secrecy and silence. They know theologically that Jesus died for their sins and that embedded in his death are the promises of forgiveness and freedom, but they simply do not know how to get from where they are to where they need to be.

They know that the hope of defeating sin is the reason Jesus came, but sexual immorality isn't just sin—you know, like lying or cheating. It's different. It's private. It's shame-inducing. It's just not something you talk about. In reality they stare at the empty cross of Jesus, and for them it seems that's exactly what it is—empty. It's empty of hope and help for them, so they live in silence. They minimize the depth of their struggle, and they determine that tomorrow they'll do better. Or they've already given up and given in, and they hope that in the end Jesus will forgive them.

In a world that has gone sexually insane, we have to do better. We have to quit being silent. We have to help one another connect the transforming power of the gospel of Jesus Christ to sex and to sexual sin and struggle. The silence must be broken. Biblical hope must be given. People need to be called out of hiding. People need to believe and act as if change really is possible. More of us need to experience the forgiveness, freedom, hope, and courage of the gospel.

That's what this chapter is about. It's meant to look at sex and sexual struggle through the hope-stimulating lens of the grace of the Lord Jesus Christ. Let's jump in.

1. You don't have to be ashamed that you're a sexual being.

We have to start here. The cross teaches us that sex is not a problem; it is a gift. Jesus didn't suffer and die to free you from sex but to free you from sexual sin. You must never give way to cursing your sexuality, because the same One who wisely created your sexuality came to be your Savior. He didn't come to fill you with guilt because you are sexual but to free you from your bondage to and guilt from sexual sin. Your sexuality points to his glory as Creator and to the amazing creature you are. It is something that the cross allows you to celebrate, because it is the grace of the cross that gives you the power to keep sex in its proper place in your heart and in your life.

Your problem and mine is not primarily that we are sexual beings; it's primarily that we tend to love the creation more than the Creator so that we use God's good gifts in ways they were not created to be used. Sexual sin and struggle are not first a matter of what we do with our body but a matter of what we do with our heart. The great Puritan teacher and preacher Richard Sibbes wrote powerfully in "The Tender Heart" of this struggle:

> Again, if you will preserve tenderness of heart, take heed of spiritual drunkenness; that is, that you be not drunk with the immoderate use of created things; of setting your love too much upon outward things. For what says the prophet, "Wine and women take away the heart" (Hosea 4:11); that is, the immoderate use of any earthly things takes away the spiritual sense; for the more sensible the soul is of outward things, the less it is of spiritual. For as the outward takes away the inward heat, so the love of one thing abates the love of another. The setting of too much love on earthly things takes away the sense of better things, and hardens the heart. When the heart is filled with the pleasures and profits of this life, it is not sensible of any judgment that hangs over the head; as in the old world, they ate and drank, they married and gave in marriage, they bought and sold, while the flood came upon them and swept all away (Matthew 24:17). When a man sets his love upon created things, the very strength of his soul is lost. . . . Talk of religion to a carnal man, whose senses are lost with the love of earthly things, he has no ear for that; his sense is quite lost, he has no relish or [savor] for anything good. Talk to a covetous man, that has his soul set upon the things of this life, he has no relish of anything else; his heart is already so hardened to get honour or wealth. Though it be to the ruin of others, that he cares not how hard it has become. Therefore we are bidden to take heed that our hearts be not overcome with drunkenness and the cares of this life, for those will make a man insensible of spiritual things (Luke 21:43).

Applying to sex what Sibbes says about the heart highlights what is important. The struggle for sexual purity is not so much a struggle with sex but with the proneness of our hearts to wander, that is, with the tendency of every sinner to look for fulfillment of heart where it cannot be found. As long as you are looking for life in the creation, you won't be seeking it in the Creator. Sex is a good and beautiful thing, but desire for this good thing becomes a bad and dangerous thing when it becomes a heart-controlling thing. The idolatry of the sinful heart is the problem. So when you ask sex to satisfy you, you have to go back again and again because the satisfaction of sex is powerful but frighteningly short-lived. Remember that asking the creation to be your savior always ends in addiction of some kind.

You don't have to be ashamed of your sexuality, but you must guard your heart as you live out your sexuality.

2. You don't have to deny that you're a sinner.
So much of what propels personal and cultural sexual insanity is active, regular, long-term self-denial. Self-righteousness is simply insane itself, but it's there in all of us. The grace of the cross of Jesus Christ means we don't have to deny reality anymore. We don't have to work to make ourselves and others think we are righteous. We don't have to recast what we have done to make it look better. We don't have to work to make acceptable to our conscience what God says is wrong. We don't have to argue that we are okay when we are not okay. Grace means we do not have to be afraid of what will be uncovered or exposed about us, because whatever is revealed has already been fully covered by the blood of Jesus.

This means that you don't have to deny your struggle for sexual purity. You don't have to act as if you're pure if you're not pure. You don't have to lie to yourself or others. You don't have to work to make lust look like something less than lust. You don't have to tell yourself that your sex life is okay when it is not okay in the eyes of God. Honesty is possible because grace is available.

Facing the depth of your sexual struggle is possible because you do not face that struggle alone; your Savior is ever with you. You and I must remember that self-denial is never a doorway to personal change. The grace of Jesus Christ welcomes you to live in the courage of honesty, knowing that there is grace for every dark and dangerous thing that will be exposed. The way you deal with your struggle for sexual purity changes when you embrace the fact that grace means you don't have to deny your struggle anymore.

But there is one more point to be made here. The Bible never presents sexual sin as being of a different nature than other sins. Sexual sin may have different social and interpersonal consequences, but it is sin, no more no less. In Romans 1 sexual sin is listed along with envy, gossip, and deceit, even with something as mundane as disobedience to parents. That is why this is important. If you begin to think that sexual sin is sin of a different kind or nature, it is logical then to wonder if the same biblical promises, hopes, and provisions apply to it.

I sat with a woman who had struggled for years with same-sex attraction, while she said to me in tears, "No one treated me as if I was just a sinner. I thought my sin was different, and what worked for others wouldn't work for me. It is wonderful to say that all sexual sin is sin—sin for which Christ died." Sexual sin sits inside the circle of the rescuing, forgiving, transforming, and delivering grace of the Lord Jesus Christ. It is a deceitful, lying enemy who would work to convince you that the provisions of the cross can't help you because sexual sin is different. In our struggle for sexual purity, each of us must reject that lie.

3. You don't have to deny the fallenness of the world around you.

You don't have to act as if life is easy and your struggles are few. You don't have to act as though you live a life free from temptation. You can admit that troubling temptation leaves you weary and sometimes confused. You can cry out for help when you are tired, distressed, or have lost the fight once again. It is right at moments to be angry at what the world around you has become. It is right to be sad that things around you are as broken as they are. You should hate the fact that sex seems to infect almost everything you encounter. You must face the fact that this right-here, right-now world will never be the paradise that your heart longs for. Paradise is coming, but this is not it.

You should be sad that the purity of your heart is always under assault by the seductive voices of evil all around. You should be angry that the sanctity and purity of your marriage must be protected because your marriage is located in a world where temptation is everywhere. It should not be okay for you. You should not grow comfortable with the sorry state of things. You should be angry that God's beautiful gift of sexuality has been so deluded and distorted. You should hate the fact that we have gone sexually crazy. And you should groan and mourn before your Savior, who hears and cares.

The words of Romans 8 are helpful to read, as Paul connects the gospel of Jesus Christ to being honest about the brokenness of the surrounding world:

> I consider that our present sufferings are not worth comparing with the glory that will be revealed in us. For the creation waits in eager expectation for the children of God to be revealed. For the creation was subjected to frustration, not by its own choice, but by the will of the one who subjected it, in hope that the creation itself will be liberated from its bondage to decay and brought into the freedom and glory of the children of God. We know that the whole creation has been groaning as in the pains of childbirth right up to the present time. Not only so, but we ourselves, who have the firstfruits of

the Spirit, groan inwardly as we wait eagerly for our adoption to sonship, the redemption of our bodies. For in this hope we were saved. But hope that is seen is no hope at all. Who hopes for what they already have? But if we hope for what we do not yet have, we wait for it patiently. In the same way, the Spirit helps us in our weakness. We do not know what we ought to pray for, but the Spirit himself intercedes for us through wordless groans. And he who searches our hearts knows the mind of the Spirit, because the Spirit intercedes for God's people in accordance with the will of God. And we know that in all things God works for the good of those who love him, who have been called according to his purpose. For those God foreknew he also predestined to be conformed to the image of his Son, that he might be the firstborn among many brothers and sisters. And those he predestined, he also called; those he called, he also justified; those he justified, he also glorified. What, then, shall we say in response to these things? If God is for us, who can be against us? He who did not spare his own Son, but gave him up for us all—how will he not also, along with him, graciously give us all things? Who will bring any charge against those whom God has chosen? It is God who justifies. Who then is the one who condemns? No one. Christ Jesus who died—more than that, who was raised to life—is at the right hand of God and is also interceding for us. Who shall separate us from the love of Christ? Shall trouble or hardship or persecution or famine or nakedness or danger or sword? As it is written:

"For your sake we face death all day long;
    we are considered as sheep to be slaughtered."

No, in all these things we are more than conquerors through him who loved us. For I am convinced that neither death nor life, neither angels nor demons, neither the present nor the

future, nor any powers, neither height nor depth, nor anything
else in all creation, will be able to separate us from the love of
God that is in Christ Jesus our Lord. (vv. 18–39 NIV)

Paul argues here that because you have been blessed with the unshakable love of the Lord Jesus Christ, you can face the struggles
of life in this fallen world with honesty and hope. Biblical faith
never requires you to deny reality. Honesty about struggles within
and temptations without is necessary if you are going to live in
sexual purity.

4. You don't have to hide in guilt and fear.

One of the saddest moments in Scripture is found in Genesis 3. For
the very first time, you find Adam and Eve hiding in fear from their
Creator. Designed for lifelong and life-shaping communion with
him, they are now afraid to face him. You know right away that
something horrible has happened. Hiding from someone whom
you say you love is never a good sign. Hiding because of guilt
and fear is a red flag that something has gone very wrong. Hiding a problem seldom leads to a solution for the problem. Lying
to others about your problem never leads to their understanding
and assistance. You hide when you tell yourself you're okay. You
hide when you minimize your struggle. You hide when you lie to
others. You hide when you give nebulous nonanswers to people
who are trying to help you. You hide when you try to cover your
struggle by making yourself look more spiritual than you are. You
hide when you convince yourself that you can do alone what you
will only ever do with the help of God and others.

The cross of Jesus Christ welcomes you out of hiding, because
on the cross Jesus endured your punishment, he carried your guilt,
he bore your shame, and he endured your rejection. He did all
this so that you wouldn't have to hide from God. He did all this

so that in your sin, weakness, and failure you could run toward a holy God and not away from him. He did all this so that you could live in the light and not lurk around in the darkness. He did all this so that you would find mercy and grace in your time of need. So step out of hiding and reach out for help. Your Savior endured the rejection you and I should have received so that even in our failure, we will never see God turn and walk away from us. Now, that's grace!

5. You don't have to fight your battle alone.

The dark secrecy of sexual sin can make you feel alienated, misunderstood, rejected, and alone. You can fall into thinking that no one will ever understand, that no one will ever want to be near you or help you. The privacy of the double life of many who are struggling with sexual sin can make them feel separated from those closest to them. If you are God's child, it is impossible for you to be alone. Let me make this distinction: it's not impossible for you to *feel* alone, but it is impossible for you to *be* alone. You and I must distinguish between the power of what we feel and the realities that should shape the way we act and respond.

Here's where the message of Scripture is so incredibly encouraging. God's greatest gift to us is the gift of himself. What changes the whole ball game is his presence. The wisdom principles of Scripture wouldn't be worth the paper they are printed on if it weren't for the powerful rescuing and transforming presence of the Redeemer. Without him with us, for us, and in us, we wouldn't understand the principles, we wouldn't desire to live inside them, and we wouldn't have the power to do so if we wanted to. Our hope for change is a person, the Lord Almighty.

You will notice as you read the Bible that every time God's people faced seemingly insurmountable difficulty, God didn't work to pump up their self-confidence. Rather, he reminded them of his presence. When God called Moses to confront Pharaoh, the most powerful ruler on earth, and Moses was afraid to go, God said, "I will be with you" (Ex. 3:12). When God called Joshua to lead Israel to defeat the warring nations of Palestine, God reminded Joshua that he was with him wherever he went (Josh. 1:5, 9). When Gideon was scared to death at the thought of leading Israel against the pirate nation of Midian, God said, "The LORD is with you" (Judg. 6:12). When God called David to be king over a defeated and divided Israel, God reminded David that he had been with him and encouraged him that he would continue (2 Sam. 7:9). When Jesus sent out his novice disciples to take the gospel to a world that didn't want it, he reminded them that he would be with them always (Matt. 28:20). And as you and I struggle with sexual purity in a world that has gone sexually insane, God says to us, "I will never leave you nor forsake you" (Heb. 13:5). As God's child it is impossible to fight the battle for purity by yourself, because you have been indwelt by a warrior Spirit who fights on your behalf, even when you don't have the sense to call on him.

But there is more. God has placed us in his church because he knows that our journey to sexual purity is a community project. We were not designed to know ourselves clearly, to identify the places where change is needed, and to fight for that change by ourselves. As Paul says in Ephesians 4:16, it is "every joint" that does its part as the body of Christ grows to maturity. If you want to be sexually pure, you need people to help you see yourself in ways that sin blinds you to. If you want to gain ground, you need people who will confront you when you are rebelling and encourage you when you are weak. And most of all, you need people who will remind you again and again of the powerful presence of your Redeemer and the lavish provisions of his grace.

You and I will never defeat sexual sin and live in restful purity if we attempt to do what we're not hardwired to do—fight the battle all by ourselves.

6. You don't have to question God's patient love.

Could there be any greater encouragement for us as we are confronted with the fickleness of our hearts, our weakness in the face of temptations, the rebellion that causes us to do what is wrong even when we know it is wrong, and the arrogance of thinking we know better than God, than the gospel declaration that nothing can separate us from the love of God in Christ Jesus? God's love is yours forever, not because you will be faithful but because he is. God's love is constant, not because you earned it in your righteousness but because God knew it was the only hope for you in your unrighteousness. God's love never wanes even when your allegiance to him does, because it is not based on your performance but on his character.

Here's the point: if you think that God's love is at stake, that he will withdraw it when you mess up, then in your moment of failure you will run from him and not to him. But if you really believe in your deepest moment of sexual foolishness, weakness, failure, or rebellion that when you run to him, he will greet you with arms of redemptive love, then it makes no sense to hide from him or to separate yourself from his care. Ultimately, in your struggle with sex, your love for God is never your hope. Hope is to be found only ever in his love for you. Since he loves you, he wants what's best for you and will work to defeat the enemies of your soul until the last enemy has been defeated and your struggle is no more.

7. You can quit thinking that change is impossible.

For all the preceding reasons, you are free to quit thinking of sexual sin as impossible to defeat. I cannot tell you the number of people I have counseled in the midst of some form of sexual struggle and functional hopelessness. They hadn't yet abandoned their formal theology, but they had lost all hope that the truths of that theology would have any impact on their lives. They had begun to succumb to the depressing perspective that what they were dealing with was impossible to defeat. In fact, some of them said something like this: "I've seen other people defeat sins in their lives, and I've seen some things change in my own, but not this one. No matter how hard I try and no matter how faithfully I pray, nothing seems to change."

But here is the truth: because what you are dealing with is sin, because that is exactly what Christ died to defeat, because you are never alone while Christ fights on your behalf, because he has blessed you with mercies that are new every morning, and because he has surrounded you with protective and restorative resources in the body of Christ, you are not encased in concrete. You can change. You can be pure. Change is not a theological fantasy. It is the bright promise of the cross of Jesus Christ. A day will come when you will struggle no more. Why not reject hopelessness and move in that direction right now?

8. You can live in a new and better way.

So if, by grace, change really is possible, then the only logical response is to get up in the morning in the courage of faith and begin to address what's broken in your sexual life. Perhaps the following questions will help you.

- Where and how do you regularly set yourself up for failure?
- Where do you tend to make foolish choices?
- Where do you expose yourself to unhelpful things?
- Where do you tend to tell yourself that you're okay when you're not?

- What things do you say to yourself that allow you to remain hopeless?
- Where do you look wrong in the face and do it anyway?
- Where and when are you most susceptible to give in to temptation?
- Where are you asking physical, sexual pleasure to satisfy your heart?
- In what ways do you tend to minimize your struggle?
- With whom are you being less than honest?
- Are there moments when you still allow yourself to question God's love?

Now, you know that addressing these questions won't rescue you from temptation and make you pure. But they can be used to help you understand your struggle, to begin to think about what a new and better way looks like, and to identify places where you need to reach out for help. In other words, the questions can function as tools in the hands of a God of glorious grace, who alone has the power to defeat sin in your life and mature you into a person pure of heart and hands.

You see, only the gospel of Jesus has the power to bring sanity to sexuality in a world gone crazy and, within this power, the potential for real, lasting, personal transformation. Yes, you can live a God-honoring sexual life in a world gone crazy. Yes, you really can.

Review and Reflect

1. How does human sexuality point to the glory of God as Creator?

2. How does the reality of God's grace free us from the need to sugarcoat our sin struggles?

3. How is sexual sin both similar to and different from other types of sin? How does the cross of Christ liberate us from guilt and fear and enable hope and obedience?

4. "God's greatest gift to us is the gift of himself" (p. 159). How does this reality empower our fight against sexual sin? Why is it crucial to include other people in our battle?

5. Write out your answers to the questions Paul Tripp poses:

   • Where and how do you regularly set yourself up for failure?

   • Where do you tend to make foolish choices?

   • Where do you expose yourself to unhelpful things?

   • Where do you tend to tell yourself that you're okay when you're not?

- What things do you say to yourself that allow you to remain hopeless?

- Where do you look wrong in the face and do it anyway?

- Where and when are you most susceptible to give in to temptation?

- Where are you asking physical, sexual pleasure to satisfy your heart?

- In what ways do you tend to minimize your struggle?

- With whom are you being less than honest?

- Are there moments when you still allow yourself to question God's love?

How do your answers help you define your personal struggle? Identify specific steps you can take to lay hold of help and hope.

Heart Reset

- Joshua 1:1–9

- Hosea 4:10–11

- Romans 8:18–39

- Hebrews 13:5

11

Sex: Are You Living
As If You're Poor?

The missionary told a compelling story, one that got my attention and still has it today. He was ministering in a horribly impoverished country to people who literally had nothing. One time as he was walking to the market to get provisions, he happened across a wandering pack of little boys. He didn't have much money himself, but his heart went out to these boys, who have little hope and a dark future ahead of them. He reached into his pocket and gave the boy who seemed to be the leader of the pack the equivalent of ten American dollars. That boy held riches in his hand that he had never imagined and would surely never see again. "Use it wisely," the missionary said as he went on his way.

After purchasing his provisions, the missionary walked home from the market along the same road. He heard the sounds of happy chatter before he saw the same pack of little boys. To his shock and surprise each of the boys had ice cream in his hand. The missionary couldn't believe what he was seeing. Immediately anger welled up inside him, and he took the leader of the pack aside and scolded him, saying, "I gave you more money than you've ever seen, and this is what you do with it?" With little hesitation the boy responded, "Sir, yesterday we were poor, tomorrow we will be poor, but today we have ice cream."

You see, poverty is not just a condition; it becomes an identity. The boy was saying, "You do get it, Mister. I am poor; I will always be poor. Your money won't keep me from being poor, so today I'll numb myself with pleasure, because I have no hope of anything ever changing." Sadly, many people who call themselves Christians and say they believe in the gospel of the Lord Jesus Christ live with a poverty mentality. They feel that they have nothing with which to face what they daily must face; they have little hope of ever having anything, so they numb themselves with the pleasures of the moment. But there is something underneath the poverty mentality.

I am convinced that there is much confusion of identity in the body of Christ. I am convinced that there are many believers who simply don't know who they are. This is significant, because every rational human being assigns some kind of identity to him- or herself. In that influential and informative self-conversation we are always having, we tell ourselves who we are. And the identity we assign to ourselves determines how we go about dealing with the stuff on our plate.

When you have *confusion of identity*, you tend to live with a *poverty mentality*, which makes you a sitting duck for *sexual insanity*. Only riches can deliver you from riches. In other words, only the heart-satisfying riches of the grace of Jesus can protect and free you from the deceptive and dissatisfying "riches" of this fallen world. Only when your heart is content can you have lasting protection against becoming addicted to the temporarily satisfying pleasures of the created world. It is vital to understand the riches you have been given in Christ. It's essential to approach life as one who is rich. It makes no sense to go out on the street and beg when you have been given an inheritance beyond your wildest dreams.

- - -

He sat slumped in the chair with his head down once again. He had the look of an utterly defeated and hopeless man. He had come to see me, but he didn't want to be there, and he had said a few things, but he had no interest in talking. No trial had brought him to this point. No, he had finally seen himself with accuracy, and what he saw had taken his breath away. He now knew that his struggles were bigger than he had ever imagined and his weakness much greater than he had assessed. After what seemed to be hours of silence but was actually less than a minute, he looked up at me and said, "I don't think I've ever felt more weak and discouraged." The moment he said it, I was relieved. He was right—his story was a chronicle of weakness. He was right—there was no hope for him all by himself.

If you can stare your personal sex insanity in the face and say, "No problem, I can handle this," then you are a person in deep spiritual trouble. Only when you are crushed by your poverty of desire, ability, and hope will you begin to get excited about the riches that are yours in the grace of the Lord Jesus Christ. And only when you daily read to yourself the gospel of those riches will you have the insight and courage to fight the battles that God calls and graces you to fight.

I knew in that moment that I would not help him by minimizing his daily temptations. I knew it wouldn't help him to negate the power of the war he was living in. I knew it wouldn't help him to pump up his assessment of his own strength. To do any of those things would have been to play into the deceptive power and attraction of sexual insanity. As I sat there with him, I was once again reminded that hopelessness is the doorway to hope. Only when we abandon our hope in our own righteousness, wisdom, and strength, and only when we abandon our hope that the created world will be our savior, will we reach out for the riches of the righteousness, wisdom, and strength found only ever in Jesus.

Who do you tell yourself you are? Do you assign to yourself riches of independent righteousness and strength you don't have? Do you assess that you are wiser than you really are? Or do you preach to yourself of your aloneness, poverty, and inability? Are you better skilled at convincing yourself that you are more hopeless than a person of robust hope? You see, both the "I can handle this" believer and the "There is no hope for someone like me" believer suffer from the same thing: *identity amnesia.* They have been saved by the blood of Jesus, but between their past forgiveness and their future in eternity, they have simply forgotten or never truly grasped who they are. So they will not seek the help they need, rest in the grace they've been given, or fight their battles with the weapons they've been given by grace.

Rich Grace

It is one of my favorite passages of Scripture. It has been a long-time friend. It gets me up in the morning. It reminds me who I am, it helps me to correctly assess what I have been given, and it gives me courage to face the battles of the day. It is one of those passages in which God paints for us a beautiful word picture:

> Come, everyone who thirsts,
>   come to the waters;
> and he who has no money,
>   come, buy and eat!
> Come, buy wine and milk
>   without money and without price.

Why do you spend your money for that which is not bread,
    and your labor for that which does not satisfy?
Listen diligently to me, and eat what is good,
    and delight yourselves in rich food.
Incline your ear, and come to me;
    hear, that your soul may live;
and I will make with you an everlasting covenant,
    my steadfast, sure love for David. (Isa. 55:1–3)

What a gorgeous picture of the heart-satisfying pleasures of grace! You will never understand who you are, what you have been given, and the resources that are yours right here, right now until you understand that as God's child you have been invited to dine at the banquet table of the King. It is an invitation you couldn't have bought. It is a meal you don't deserve. Yours is food you couldn't have earned. Only when you get who you are and the table that grace has put your feet under will you quit trying to feed your soul on what will never satisfy. Only resting in the riches you have been given will free you from seeking riches where they cannot be found. Only a full and satisfied heart is free from the insanity of a ravenous heart. Only when you are eating with joy the food of the King will you quit seeking food elsewhere. Only when you rest in the reality that you have been given life will you quit looking to sex satisfaction to give you life. When you begin to understand that you've been invited to a meal that will never end, that you've been welcomed to the King's table forever, you'll quit looking to sneak a bite at other tables.

The Rich Food of Redemption

So what does it actually look like to affirm your identity as a child of God and live in light of his lavish resources of grace? What does it mean to approach the struggle of sex from the perspective of the gospel of Jesus Christ? What new ways of living would result from truly believing that you have been welcomed to the soul-satisfying banquet table of the King of kings? What is the right-here, right-now gospel that each of us must preach to ourselves every day to protect ourselves from the sex insanity that is often inside us and everywhere around us? Below is a starting place.

1. I am never alone.

In your struggle for God-honoring stewardship of your body and the purity of your heart, you must tell yourself again and again that if you're God's child, if you have been redeemed by his grace, and if you have been welcomed into his eternal family, it is absolutely impossible to ever be alone. There is no situation, no relationship, no location, and no struggle in which you exist all by yourself. No, your life has been invaded by the Savior, the King, the Lamb, the Captain, the victor Jesus Christ. He is your spiritual life. He is your power, your wisdom, and your hope. He is the food and the drink at the King's table. God's most wonderful gift to us is not a thing—it is a person. Our need was so great, our battle with sin so profound, that he knew the only thing that would help us was himself. So he gave us himself in the gift of his crucified, resurrected, and indwelling Son.

This means I can no longer look at my life and my struggles with sex in a "me against the world" way. I cannot allow myself to assess my potential to defeat the next temptation based on my previous track record and the size of the thing I am facing. I can't go around thinking that I've been left to my ingenuity and strength. This kind of thinking denies the gospel realities of who I am and what I have been given. The presence of the Lord with me always belies any personal assessments of aloneness or inability.

Now, this reality of his presence seems counterintuitive. Doubt, fear, anxiety, envying another's life, wondering if you have what it takes, and wishing life were easier are natural; but living in light of the constant presence of the Redeemer isn't. This is why it is so important to preach this truth to yourself again and again.

2. I have all the resources I need.

The apostle Paul says that God has "blessed us in Christ with every spiritual blessing" (Eph. 1:3). He also ends his discussion in Romans 8 about life in the fallen world with these words: "He who did not spare his own Son but gave him up for us all, how will he not also with him graciously give us all things?" (v. 32). Peter writes to suffering and struggling people these encouraging words: "His divine power has granted to us all things that pertain to life and godliness" (2 Pet. 1:3). Yes, God has chosen to keep us here for a time, where the full range of the temptations of sex insanity exists and in some way greets us every day. Yes, we still live in a world where the Devil lurks about as a ravenous beast. And it is true that between the already and the not yet we still carry inside ourselves the susceptibility to sin. But it is not true that we have been left on our own without any resources.

Grace means that God will not leave you on your own, and he will never call you to a situation or location without giving you what you need, to do what he has called you to do. So I must at times flee, and there are times when I must stand and resist. I must avoid the tendency to name myself as more wise, righteous, and strong than I actually am. I must resist the dark lie of the Enemy that comes to me in a variety of forms and seeks to get me to believe that life can be found outside of the Savior. I must fight the draw to look for heart satisfaction in a thing like sexual pleasure. I must deal with my temptation to love the creation more than I do the Creator. I must always watch what I surrender my heart to. But I do none of these things in my own power or with my own resources. I can stand and affirm that I have no power on my own to either resist or defeat sin and be perfectly at rest, because I have been blessed with the rich resources of amazing grace. I don't have to hope that I'll have what I need. No, the cross assures me that I already have in my personal spiritual storehouse everything I could ever need. Could it be possible to preach this to yourself too much?

3. I am forgiven.

What often drives the sex struggles underground, giving room for sin to do its ugly work, is the powerful triad of self-righteousness, guilt, and shame. First, in an act of irrationality I attach my inner sense of well-being to my own righteousness, forgetting that the best of my righteousness is like a filthy rag, so I try to prove to God and myself and demonstrate to others that I am righteous. Because of this, I minimize, deny, excuse, rationalize, or shift the blame for my sin. I work to make myself feel good about what is not good. I recast my own history, and I rewrite my own stories, all for the purpose of self-atonement. Meanwhile the insanity of sex attraction, temptation, and addiction are growing in my heart.

Or I panic in the face of the clear sex-struggle evidence that I am not righteous at all. I give way to fear because I blow it in big and small ways again and again. And in moments when I am not acting out, I am constantly attracted to or desiring things that I should not. I cannot escape the guilt of my street-level unfaithfulness and am not able to make it all look okay. So I hide in shame, fearing the rejection of others and the anger of God. I cannot believe that God could place his love on a person like me. This too is a function of debilitating self-righteousness that completely forgets the gospel of Jesus Christ.

It doesn't matter how exotically righteous you are. It doesn't matter how pure you are in your dealings with sex. It doesn't matter how strong you are against temptation. Your standing with

God is never based on your righteousness, but on his. His perfect life, his acceptable death, and his death-defeating resurrection guaranteed your standing with God. All your sins—past, present, and future—have been covered by his blood. His righteousness has been attributed to your account. So even in your moment of greatest failure, you do not have to hide from God or fear his presence. Your penalty has been paid and eternal acceptance has been granted, so you can run into God's presence, lost and broken as you often are, without fear of his rejection. Grace guarantees your forgiveness, pays the penalty for your guilt, and lifts the burden of shame off your shoulders. You simply can't preach forgiveness to yourself too often.

4. There is someone who understands me.

The writer of Hebrews assures us with these words: "We do not have a high priest who is unable to sympathize with our weaknesses, but one who in every respect has been tempted as we are, yet without sin" (Heb. 4:15). In writing these words, the author exposes one of the cruel lies of the Enemy. This lie is meant to paralyze you as you seek to battle the myriad of sexual temptations that regularly greet you. The lie goes this way: "No one understands what you're going through because no one is dealing with what you're dealing with." This lie is not only fashioned to get you to embrace the discouraging thought that no one could ever understand you, but it is also designed to do something even more debilitating. It is designed to get you to doubt the goodness of God. Here is the underbelly of this lie: "No one will understand you, because you have been singled out. Look around you—no one is going through what you've been going through. Maybe God has forgotten you. Maybe he is not always there. Perhaps he does, in fact, have favorites. Maybe he doesn't always answer prayer." All this is meant to get you to doubt God's goodness, because if you don't trust his character in your moments of sexual temptation, you won't run to him for help.

But the writer of Hebrews says that the exact opposite is true. In a grace-driven desire that you would have just the right help in your moment of sex-struggle need, Jesus exposed himself to every kind of temptation you face so that you would always know that you seek help from one who knows exactly what you're going through. And because he knows exactly what you're going through, he is able to offer help that is form-fit for you and for the battle of the moment. So you don't have to give way to the hesitation of doubt. No, you can go to him with complete confidence. He knows, he understands, and he greets you with the sympathy of someone who has not only been there but has defeated what you now need to defeat. Wow! There is not a day when you and I don't need to hear this.

5. Change is possible for me.

All this means that no matter now many times I have failed, how many times I have said yes to what required a no, or how defeated I feel, I am not stuck; change really is possible. My existence has been taken over and altered by powerful, zealous, and unstoppable grace. No matter how great my sin, no matter how foolish I am, and no matter how messy my track record, grace will ultimately win. God's kingdom will come. His will will be done. He will not relent until every microbe of sin is delivered from every cell of every heart of every one of his children.

In our battle with sex insanity, you and I are blessed to be the sons and daughters of a zealous and dissatisfied Redeemer. He doesn't get discouraged. He doesn't panic when things are hard. He doesn't wonder if he made the wrong choice in placing his grace on you. He doesn't wring his hands and wish the problem would go away. He won't give up with the job half done. And he surely won't drop his work in you and walk away. You can change, not because you have the right motives or the right amount of power, but because he will not sit down until the final enemy has been defeated.

You and I simply cannot allow ourselves to give way to the paralysis of hopelessness. Yes, there will be moments when change does look impossible. There will be times when it seems that things are getting worse, not better. There will be times when we will be tempted to wonder if God is there and if he is who he has declared himself to be. There will be times when we'll wonder if grace has forgotten our address. But we must remember that our Redeemer is not like us. He would never, ever consider forsaking the work of his hands. He is covenantally committed to completing in us what he has begun. Our hope for change rests not so much on our character but on his. Now, that's good news!

6. Weakness is not my big problem, but my delusion of strength is.

Here are paradigm-changing words, words that are designed to revolutionize what you think about yourself and life in this fallen world: "My grace is sufficient for you, for my power is made perfect in weakness" (2 Cor. 12:9). When you think you're strong, or when you work to make yourself believe you're strong, you won't seek and rest in the powerful grace you have been given in Christ Jesus. We all just need to get a grip. Our stories present ample evidence that we are, in fact, quite weak, and in our weakness, quite susceptible to surrendering to things we should resist. We have all given way to sexual temptations that we should have run from. But we needn't panic. God knows just how weak we are. He is not shocked or surprised by the evidence of our lack of power. No, his grace isn't thwarted by our weakness. The opposite is true: his grace does its best work precisely at the moment our weaknesses have been exposed.

You see, our hope rests not in the size of our strength but in the inestimable magnitude of his. Grace can deal with all our weaknesses, but when we tell ourselves that we're strong, we have little interest in that grace. It would do all of us a whole lot of good to listen to the message that our struggle with sex preaches. There are few areas in our lives that preach a gospel of neediness more than our struggles with sexual purity of heart and hands. If you listen to that message, you will be a seeker and celebrator of the powerful grace that has been lavished on you.

7. I have been given rich wisdom for daily living.

One of the sad effects of sin is that it shrinks all of us to fools. We don't need any more evidence of the foolishness of sin in the stupid choices human beings make than what we do with sex. Consider King David's adultery with Bathsheba. What was he thinking? In his mind, what was the end game? What did he imagine God would do? Did he really think he would get away with it? How did he convince himself that this illicit relationship was okay and would end okay? What a powerful picture of the foolishness of sin.

Foolishness is the problem of every human being because it is one of the inescapable effects of sin, and we are all sinners. We cannot escape this foolishness, because we cannot escape ourselves. So it is here that the gospel of Jesus Christ greets us with such power. The gospel declares that wisdom is not first a book, a blog post and tweet, or a theological essay. No, wisdom is first a person, and his name is Jesus. Paul says in Colossians 2:3 that Jesus is the one "in whom are hidden all the treasures of wisdom and knowledge." To rescue us from our foolishness, God gave us the only thing that would help—his Son.

But not only have we been given the Son, who is the Word;

also we have been blessed with the Word of the Son. Every page of Scripture gives us wisdom that we do not have on our own. There are things you need to know as you struggle with sex insanity, things you would never know by means of personal experience and collective research. These vital truths are known only by means of revelation.

God gifts us with his Word so that we may know him and his plan, so that we may understand ourselves and our needs, and so that we may know where lasting hope and help can be found. The purpose of God's Word is not so much religious and theological information but personal transformation. So the Son, who is the Word, and the Word of the Son mean that we are not left to our own foolishness. There is One who is wisdom, who gifts us with wisdom we would never, ever have without him. We need to tell this to ourselves again and again.

8. Only the riches of grace satisfy my heart.

I don't need to say much more about this, other than to repeat that this is a truth we need to preach to ourselves every day. You and I will only ever get vertically the heart satisfaction we all seek. It simply cannot and will not be found horizontally. Every created thing is without the capacity to satisfy your heart. The created world was designed to point you to where your heart will find its contentment and rest: in God and God alone. The sex insanity that harms and/or destroys our lives is the result of seeking from creation what can be found only at the foot of the Creator.

9. It's guaranteed that my struggle with sex will end.

The victory of Jesus assures your victory. In farming terms, he is the firstfruits. The appearance of the first apple on the tree is a guarantee of more apples to come. The empty cross and the tomb of Jesus are your guarantee that your sexual temptation, sin, and addiction will someday be defeated, and you will live forever and be free of internal and external insanity. That guarantee of its future defeat is also a guarantee of all the grace you need along the way.

Yes, we do live in a world that has gone sex insane. And, yes, that insanity still lives in some way in all our hearts. But we needn't panic; we needn't succumb; we needn't think that our battles are leading nowhere. We must not give way to assessments of poverty, aloneness, and impossibility, because the insanity has been invaded by the Messiah, Jesus. He faced every insane thing we face, and he defeated it all on our behalf. He did all this so that you and I would have the grace we need to face the sexual struggles we will continue to face until eternity is our home and the insanity has been quieted forever.

Review and Reflect

1. "The identity we assign to ourselves determines how we go about dealing with the stuff on our plate" (p. 168). How does this truth play out?

2. How does acknowledging personal weakness actually produce strength? See 2 Corinthians 12:7–10.

3. Reread Isaiah 55:1–3. How does this passage impact your thinking about your sex life?

4. The gospel of Jesus Christ can reshape our identity—including our sexual identity. Explain how the gospel truths laid out in chapter 11 alter your thinking. Which of the nine truths Paul outlines impact you most deeply and why?

5. Sexual insanity has been invaded by the Messiah. How is Jesus Christ the only path to sexual sanity?

Heart Reset

- Isaiah 55:1–3

- 2 Corinthians 12:7–10

- Ephesians 1:3–10

- Hebrews 4:14–15

- 2 Peter 1:2–4

General Index

Adam and Eve, 71–72; and the fall, 72, 76; and the garden of Eden, 45, 71, 74–75; and God's boundaries, 74

addiction, 75–76; the dynamic of, 34–35, 154; sexual, 35, 37

antinomianism, 105–6

asceticism, 71; chief worldview of, 71; etiology of the word, 71; misunderstanding of the nature of God's creation and of human beings, 71–72

authority, 133–36; God's authority, 134; human authority, 134; mistaken Western philosophical view of, 75

big-picture sex, 88, 98; connected to God's eternity, 96–97; connected to God's existence, 91–92; connected to God's glory, 92–93; connected to God's purpose, 93–74; connected to God's redemption, 95–96; connected to God's revelation, 94–95

boundaries, God's setting of, 45–46, 74–75; and Adam and Eve, 74

bowing down, 49

brokenness, 16–20, 95, 155–58. See also suffering

change, 161–62, 176–77; helpful questions for facilitation of, 162–63

church, the, 160

confession: David's prayer of (Psalm 51), 64–66; to God, 64, 126, 144, 145; relational, 129

creation, 44; and the concepts of design and ownership, 44; and the Creator-creature distinction, 45–46; as penultimate, 92. See also creation, implications of

creation, implications of, 41–42; all of life is spiritual, 46–48; God as center of all things, 42–44; God as creator and owner of all that exists, 44–46; God is worthy of our worship, 49–50

David: adultery of with Bathsheba, 178; God's presence with, 160; prayer of confession (Psalm 51), 64–66

deception, 62–63

delay, 140–41

desire, 114

Devil, the, 173; lies of, 23, 114, 173, 175; temptation of Eve, 76

disobedience, 141–43; as a condition of the heart, 141; and ownership posture, 141–42; and self-swindling, 142–43

Scripture Index